HISTORICALLY BLACK COLLEGES AND UNIVERSITIES' GUIDE TO EXCELLENCE

T0281967

HISTORICALLY BLACK COLLEGES AND UNIVERSITIES' GUIDE TO EXCELLENCE

WILLIAM R. HARVEY

AMISTAD

An Imprint of HarperCollins*Publishers*

HarperCollins books may be purchased for educational, business, or sales
promotional use. For information, please email the Special Markets Department at SPsales@harpercollins.com.

FIRST EDITION

Designed by Janet Evans-Scanlon

Library of Congress Cataloging-in-Publication Data has been applied for.

ISBN 978-0-06-286328-7

23 24 25 26 27 LBC 5 4 3 2 1

This book is dedicated to the great leaders of HBCUs throughout history. A few of the giants I was fortunate to know and interact with personally were Dr. Johnetta B. Cole (Spelman College), Dr. Norman C. Francis (Xavier University), Dr. Luther H. Foster (Tuskegee University), Dr. Arthur D. Gray (Talladega College), Dr. Martin D. Jenkins (Morgan State University), and Dr. Benjamin E. Mays (Morehouse College). These individuals and others were educators, humanitarians, ministers, civil rights activists, businessmen and -women, and philanthropists who took courageous stands for desegregation and the rights of African Americans. I marvel at how diligently they worked toward excellence without compromising their principles.

I salute them with this dedication. These individuals helped establish the firm foundation and strong legacy of the HBCU community.

CONTENTS

THE INHERITANCE

After more than fifty years of experience working in leadership at historically Black colleges and universities (HCBUs), I have learned a great many things about what makes our institutions so incredible and unique. Our schools are not only homes for education, but they are an inheritance of our people. I consider historically Black colleges and universities to be the birthright of Black people everywhere. While HBCUs offer exceptional education to people from all walks of life, they are the homes of our nation's Black history. It is impossible to tell the story of American history without including the history of historically Black colleges and universities. It is likewise impossible to understate how powerful these schools are, and what they mean for our culture, and our future. My belief in this fact is what has driven me to work diligently and earnestly over four decades at Hampton University. I can only pray that my work honors the legacy of this prestigious institution that we affectionately call our "Home by the Sea."

Attending an HBCU is like learning that your long-lost ancestor has passed on and left you a huge inheritance. Then you learn that your uncle is Frederick Douglass. Or Booker T. Washington. Or W. E. B. Du Bois. Or that your aunt is Toni Morrison, or Barbara Jordan, or Katherine Johnson. These are only a handful of names to be cited among a panoply of great figures in our history who were shaped and trained at historically Black institutions.

HBCUs were founded to meet an important need. There were generations of Blacks denied an education during slavery. These individuals did not have an opportunity to receive any formal learning, much less the privilege of attending an HBCU. When HBCUs were founded in the 1800s, former slaves were some of their biggest supporters because they understood the importance of an education. One such supporter was abolitionist Frederick Douglass, who taught himself to read and write.

Known for his writings and oratory skills, Douglass traveled the country and the world as an abolitionist, advocating for the freedom of slaves. After the Civil War, which led to the slaves being freed, Douglass continued to speak about the future of the freed slaves. Some of these speeches were given on the campuses of HBCUs, including Hampton University. On his visit to Hampton, Douglass wrote:

> This school is too vast, too multiform, too cosmian, to be grasped in a single hour. I have seen London, I have seen Edinburgh, I have seen Venice, I have seen the Coliseum, I have seen the British Museum, but I should not have seen the world if I had not seen Hampton Institute.

I have seen more today of what touches my feelings, more of prophecy of what is to be, more of contrast with what has been, than I have ever seen before. . . . I feel profound pleasure, my young friends, in looking upon this glorious view, looking up to this beaming sky, and thinking of the benevolent kindness; the disinterested, lofty, religious sentiment, out of which these buildings have sprung; out of which Huntington Hall has sprung, and all these work shops for your training in useful arts—the joiner shop, the shops for the workers of wood, the workers of leather, the printing office—I can't talk, I can only say I am glad-glad-glad deep in my heart, with what I see.

> Frederick Douglass [January 1884]
> (Feb. 1884, *Southern Workman*, Vol. 13:14)

The world does not always recognize the legacy of our schools in their fullness, but I can say confidently that our institutions are havens for Black excellence, innovation, and success. They are the foundation of our advancement as Black people both here in the United States and all over the world. So, when a young Black student steps foot on our campuses and brings their talent and curiosity to the hallowed grounds and classrooms, this is what I like to think of as a homecoming. Our students come home to the physical and ideological birthplaces of Black culture and thought in America.

The greatest contribution that I believe HBCUs offer to their students, and to all who benefit from our influences both directly and indirectly, is a chance to study, learn, and interact based on merit and humanity, and not on the basis of race. Race is a constant qualifier in our world, and it touches nearly every aspect of our lives explicitly or implicitly. Racial categorization is not something that we as Black people constructed for ourselves—race is a construct of control, imperialism, and oppression. Through hard-won battles for sovereignty and self-actualization, we have developed our own identities, and established institutions that serve and cater to who we are. So, in our institutions, blackness is not a thing to hide or be ashamed of. Blackness is not a shackle, and it is not a marker of inferiority. Blackness is not an obstacle to education, or to success, inherently. HBCUs offer the opportunity for their students to transcend the racial barriers of the outside world, and to be better equipped to handle them when they graduate. Scholars can explore who they are outside of the paradigm of what blackness ought to be and whom it ought to serve. To be free enough to seek out one's own interests, and to fully pursue them with support, encouragement, and ample resources in hand, is a privilege. There is nowhere on the lands of this nation where that privilege for Black people is more protected and cherished than at historically Black universities. The heritage of our schools is one of life, liberty, and the pursuit of happiness for all people. This is why our schools were built, and this is why they continue to provide and perform despite great adversity throughout time.

Freedom from the burden of racial judgments makes for better, more authentic learning. A robust education is the foundation for a long and successful career. What today we call "Black excellence" was born at the Black college. Some might think it presumptuous of me to say so, but I don't believe it is. For what would our world look like today if W. E. B. Du Bois had not received his education at Fisk University? Or if Booker T. Washington, one of the most influential African Americans during his time, had not left Hampton Institute and founded Tuskegee Institute? Or if the great Ida B. Wells had not earned her schooling from Rust College and Fisk? Would the NAACP, a seminal organization for the rights of all people, especially colored people, have been so successful and influential in our nation? What would our world look like without the vast literary contributions of writers like Langston Hughes, Ta-Nehisi Coates, Alice Walker, and Nikki Giovanni? What would be the state of our nation's legal and political systems without the efforts of trailblazers like Thurgood Marshall, Ella Baker, Anna Julia Cooper, and John C. Lewis? Our sitting vice president, Kamala Harris, is a graduate of Howard University, and it brings me immense pride to know that the first-ever Black person to hold such a position is the product of a historically Black university.

It is true that HBCUs make up only 3 percent of the nation's schools but educate nearly 20 percent of Black graduates. HBCUs produce 25 percent of all African American STEM graduates, and the majority of Black teachers, physicians, and lawyers earn their undergraduate degrees from HBCUs. Punching above their weight, our institutions achieve all of this while serving individuals from all income levels, including the most statistically marginalized demographic in this country—poor African Americans.

HBCUs offer Black students experiences that they may never have been offered before, in a way that they have likely never witnessed before. They offer rich history, and a documented precedent of Black excellence that inspires and enables students to work confidently in pursuit of their dreams. They offer lifelong community, which allows for exchange of ideas, knowledge, and understanding, as well as support for students who otherwise would be overlooked or underestimated in other settings. They offer values, which act as guiding tools for graduates as they navigate the working world with an unapologetically Black-affirming perspective. Finally, they offer a sense of safety, which is impossible to understate when we think of how hostility and incivility can undermine a person's self-worth and education.

The inheritances of HBCUs are for everyone, and the lessons one learns at these schools can be translated and reproduced in all types of circumstances and communities. There is no universal way to be a Black person, or a Black graduate, and so while I believe that most every Black student could find value in an HBCU experience, each person has the right to choose the best educational opportunities for him- or herself. I only hope that when Black students graduate from their university of choice, they are equipped with the tools and confidence they need to take on the world and charge toward their goals. Topics tackled in this book, like character, work ethic, vision, and service, are universal concepts that can be learned anywhere. However, what I know about these lessons from the lens of an HBCU alumnus and leader is what I hope can be a worthy offering to those seeking a proud and race-conscious take on the rules of success.

What we know about HBCUs, beyond the magic that they create within their walls and campuses, is that they are homes for visionaries, missionaries, and trailblazers. Ideas birthed on HBCU campuses inevitably encounter the rest of the nation, and sometimes the globe, be it through education, innovation, or activism. Like seeds traveling to new worlds and planted by brave hands into new lands, the wisdom and inheritance of historically Black colleges and universities continue to propagate and bear fruit. I hope that you find some harvest in the pages of this book, and that you take part in the inheritance of our people from this day forward.

GOOD CHARACTER

Spiritual Tools for a Material World

My spirituality is important to me, and I often come back to biblical lessons whenever I need guidance or a little inspiration. In my opinion, cultivating good character is more about a person's spiritual outlook than their physical or material conditions. We all know lots of people who have great attitudes and reputations but few means and resources. Likewise, it's easy to name people and institutions with immense wealth and no moral fiber whatsoever. You can't smell or taste a person's character, but you can sure see, hear, and feel it. This is because these seemingly intangible aspects of a person's being are manifested in the way they live their lives.

When I think of character, my mind immediately goes to the traits of honesty, integrity, trustworthiness, respect for oneself and others, and responsible personal behavior. Having good character is important, no matter your age, stage in life, race, sex, or socioeconomic status, or if you live in a rural or urban community. It is always timely and priceless, and it is essential to a life well-lived.

Good character opens doors, breaks down walls, and is an investment in a better future. With good character and reputation, you can gain access to rooms and opportunities that you may not ever have anticipated. When hardship comes, or you are met with a closed door, or worse, a wall that seems impenetrable and impossible to breach, good character will give you the strength to break barriers and complete the work and tasks at hand with confidence and optimism. Finally, good character is like storing savings away for the future. What you cultivate today in character, you will reap later in success.

I have learned so much about good character and personal growth through lessons in the good book, and I hope that no matter your religious or spiritual beliefs, you will also be able to glean some insight from the words I share in this chapter.

"Character Produces Hope"

Being good for goodness's sake doesn't seem to be in style these days. It may be a great motto for children awaiting Santa Claus, but a lot of people don't see the point in acting morally unless something is in it for them. While I can't say I understand this line of thinking, I do believe that just like anything else in life, what you put in is what you get out. That means that what we put into our character and the time spent investing in our personal development will always produce a reward. So, for those who need some incentives to keep striving toward a better self, I share this passage from Romans 5:3–5 in the New Testament:

"Suffering produces endurance, endurance produces character, character produces hope, and hope does not put us to shame. . . ."

What I appreciate most in these short few phrases is the clearly defined origin and progress of character that leads to the fruit it produces. We may not always like it, but character is often built through hard times and struggle. The word *suffering* here may conjure up an unpleasant history, but I like to think of suffering in this context as the endurance of discomfort for a particular purpose. While discipline and training may be unpleasant, being able to navigate through trying situations over time will help to build our character. This is because good character is cultivated. It can't be purchased or cheaply manufactured. You won't find it on the shelf at the supermarket or in your Amazon shopping cart. Good character is organic and homegrown, and it takes time to develop.

Through the endurance of sometimes uncomfortable situations, your character will grow strong, like an athlete's body that has been put through physical rigor for the purpose of developing strength. Endurance and perseverance are part of the proving process for developing good character. In the end, the "suffering" provides spiritual strength and fortitude. Good character is the muscle we use to make it through challenges and to find success in all endeavors.

Hope is also cited in this verse, and I always find this to be a truly refreshing insight on the power and utility of good character. Hope can be a hard thing to nail down, and it sometimes seems impossible to attain. We can easily look around at all the trouble, war, injustice, and hardship in the world and become discouraged or defeated. It's hard to imagine that working to build a strong sense of character would have anything to do with hope. Yet, I have come to understand this to be true! Developing the tools and strengthening the skills we need to be ready for trials does indeed make us more hopeful. I think this is because when we are prepared for the challenge, we can be more optimistic about the outcome. When we are confident in our ability to withstand and endure difficulty, our resolve is reinforced by the strength of our character, and we are more capable in our efforts than if we were unprepared. Hope is a powerful product of character, and a much-needed resource in our world. Furthermore, as stated in this verse, hope does not disappoint us, or put us to shame. Hope provides dignity in difficult situations, and optimism inspires pride in one's ability to succeed. As a final product in the equation of endurance and character, hope offers us a chance to be successful and proud, in any and all circumstances.

The Elements of Good Character: Truth, Honesty, Integrity, Loyalty, Trust, and Justice

Especially when we consider the challenges that Black communities face in this country, and around the world, it is clear to me that more positive influences and character-building experiences are necessary. Systemic violence, disenfranchisement, discrimination, and injustice compounded over centuries are bound to have a negative influence on a people. These negative influences are often internalized in vulnerable communities, and this produces poor character in too many of our young people. How can we counteract this phenomenon, and restore values of righteousness, honesty, humility, and pride? I believe it starts with working to restore good character to its rightful guiding position in the Black community.

The forces that maintain injustice and cement a sense of disempowerment for our people ought to be challenged, and, as the good Reverend Dr. Martin Luther King Jr. once said, "The arc of the moral universe is long, but it bends toward justice."

Change may take some time to come, but it does happen! Furthermore, it doesn't happen while we are waiting for someone else to see the dignity, purpose, and power within us! We ought to hold ourselves to our own high standards, regardless of what may be expected of us from the powers that be. Good character is even more critical and necessary where great hardships are being endured. It is often difficult to face up to the injustices of this world, but it is virtually impossible to do so without preparation. Good character is the armor that protects us in our battle for a better world.

TRUTH

The foundation of good character is a personal relationship with truth. This relationship is more than simply knowing right from wrong, or being on the right side of the law, or even the court of public opinion. In this age of fast news and media, it has become incredibly apparent just how subjective "truth" can be. Today, truth is tweaked, spun, and manipulated to fortify agendas made by people who want to make money and establish power over others. A lot of young people I encounter have become quite disillusioned about the truth. They don't believe in objective truth, and I must admit that our current political climate is more ensnared in division and misinformation today than it was when I was a young man. However, I know that hope for a world in which integrity and good character prevail is not lost. Despite what some politicians and the polarized media would like you to believe, manipulations of the truth cannot endure forever. A proper relationship with truth, in which a person allows the truth to guide and shape their lives, will never go out of style. Truth is classic, dependable, and evergreen. Employing truth as a central value of your life will always prove the best choice in the end.

HONESTY

Honesty is a person's first relationship to truth, and honesty is first and foremost about being able to tell the truth to oneself. Being honest with ourselves is most important because the lies that we tell others are lies that we have told ourselves first. Likewise, being honest with ourselves enables us to be honest with others. When we are honest with ourselves, we can have greater clarity on who we are and what we are about. It helps us to determine what is right for us, where our values lie, and even determines our strengths and weaknesses. When we lie to others about these things, it is usually because we have already lied to ourselves and feel that we must now trick others and obfuscate the truth even further.

I'm sure we can all think of someone in our lives whose penchant for dishonesty causes trouble not only for others around them, but for themselves as well. Some of us *are* that person, and admittedly, we all have been that person in some moment or another. It is easy to be deceived into thinking that bending the truth for our benefit will never catch up with us, especially when we get away with it! Some people lie and never get caught. Some people commit deplorable acts and are never held accountable or brought to justice. However, the repercussions of dishonesty manifest most greatly within ourselves, and we are the first ones to hear the lies that come from our mouths. If we are dishonest with others, it is unlikely that we will be able to be honest with ourselves. If we are unable to be honest with ourselves, we risk remaining stuck in old patterns and cycles that impede our growth.

I find that being honest with myself is most useful when I am facing challenges or learning how to be better in specific situations. It is important to be able to self-assess, to learn from your mistakes and make positive adjustments whenever necessary. It's very hard to do these things if you are not being honest about your weaknesses and failings. Growth and development require candid assessment. You must have the humility and courage to tell yourself the truth in order to evolve and change.

Being honest with ourselves is also a useful tool for clarifying our values and making wise decisions. We can find peace and resolve in challenging situations when we know that we have been honest with ourselves, and consequently with others. We don't have to manipulate the truth or people-please when we are standing in our truth. We don't have to hide our real feelings or live in the balance of other people's opinions when we are being honest with ourselves. When we know we are walking in truth, we can make choices that reflect who we really are and what we really believe.

INTEGRITY

Integrity is another aspect of being honest with ourselves, and living out a daily application of the truth. In a way, integrity is how we show respect to ourselves and to our values. We must all develop our own standards for living and use our common sense and judgement to establish the kind of people we are to be, and the kind of life we are to live.

Integrity is the glue that holds a person's character together, and it is an integral component of good character. Without integrity, honesty means nothing. As the Bible says, "If I know the good I ought to do, and do not do it, I have sinned."

It is not enough to know the truth but to live it. This means doing what is right, not simply what might be most popular, or expedient. Especially when we are over-concerned with the opinions of others, we are more likely to betray ourselves and make poor decisions. However, when we live with integrity, we honor ourselves and our values. Living with integrity means deciding to let truth and righteousness guide us. When we decide to live and work with integrity, we eventually develop a reputation for being honorable and trustworthy.

LOYALTY AND TRUST

The reputations that we earn are a direct reflection of our character and our integrity. When we honor ourselves by living according to the high standards we have chosen, we can become dependable members of our communities. Loyalty and trust are ways in which honesty operates in community. I believe that the more honest we are with ourselves and with others, the more trust that we gain from our friends, family, and community. With trust we develop loyalty, and with loyalty, we are able to establish relationships that strengthen communal bonds. Loyalty is also about being accountable to others and being able to count on others. This is another reason why a person's personal relationship to the truth is so very important. When we lie and deceive others, we disrespect ourselves and those who have placed their trust in us. For this very reason, getting caught in a lie is one of the most embarrassing things that can happen to a person's reputation. Rebuilding trust where it has been lost is not simple, and the shameful exposure of moral impropriety is difficult to recover from.

Though complicated at times, we can always recommit to truth and to the rebuilding of trust with others. When trust is broken or lost, repairing relationships is all about acknowledging harm and committing to a change in behavior. Just as knowing the truth is meaningless if we do not live in the truth, promises of change are meaningless without a real transformation of our actions. Without accountability, our social standards degrade, and justice becomes difficult to achieve.

Acknowledging our shortcomings and asking for forgiveness is a skill that requires humility and courage. Likewise, extending forgiveness to those who have breached our trust can be equally daunting for our character. In this age of "cancel culture," holding others accountable can sometimes turn into holding others hostage to their own mistakes.

JUSTICE

I would be remiss if I did not find a way to include a sense of justice in this discussion on character. I believe that justice in our society hinges on being honest *and* gracious with one another. In this balance, we can find the truth and maintain our values as a society and within our communities.

Having a sense of justice is fundamental to living with good character and according to a standard. Without an awareness of justice, we become callous and self-serving, and we lose sight of why the truth is so important. Cultivating a sense of justice means being committed to truth in collective action. Justice is a principle of fairness, and it ought to be based upon what is right, fair, and honest. When unfairness happens, obfuscation of the truth allows people to shirk responsibility and burden the public with the repercussions of injustice. We cannot have real justice without a commitment to the truth. Truth is not always objective, not always black and white in an easily definable way. However, a commitment to honoring the truth remains the only way we can respond to unfairness and harm, and to ensure that our societies are guided by what is right—not what is popular or what is in our selfish interests, but what is truly the best outcome given the situation at hand.

A Word on Influence

When we consider character, it is equally important to remember the power of influence. Influence is a significant part of the equation because forces of influence are acting at all times to shape our character, whether we are aware of it or not. The tech and marketing companies have figured this out and have built entire industries of influence through media and social networking programs. Young entrepreneurs and self-proclaimed "influencers" strike deals with brands to use their lifestyles as living advertisements and to help sway opinions and trends. Litigation is waged and enormous sums of money are exchanged every day over government's and businesses' rights to influence your mind, your attitudes, and your decision-making. Influence is a determining factor in character, and that means that we must be selective and wise when choosing the forces that will have access to our inner lives.

Because influences, both positive and negative, are always working to shape us, it is not a question of whether a person's character will develop, but rather a question of how! As children, we are most directly influenced by our parents and family members. They control the types of experiences we have and the degree to which we are exposed to positive or negative character-building opportunities. We are also influenced by our communities and the physical and social environment of our homes. What we see around us is most readily adopted and integrated by our impressionable young minds.

Although childhood experiences are a strong determining factor in the outcomes of our adult lives, I believe that no matter a person's background or foundational experiences, there always exist opportunities to be transformed and to be influenced by new things. One must simply remain open to wisdom and inspiration.

For many, higher education offers the chance for new things to enter our lives. No matter what background you come from, and how many or few positive influences you have had in your life, there is always room for evolution and improvement. Some students come to a university having all the work ethic and ambition necessary to excel academically but need experience in the social aspect of college life. Through their experiences, they will learn the value of soft skills, building networks, and finding the right connections to expand their views and advance their careers. Others may come to campus with good social skills. They may have charisma, passion, and lots of hope for their future, but they need to learn how to channel all these talents through a work ethic and discipline to be successful. There are hundreds of different possible variations, but the greater point to take here is that we all have strengths and weaknesses, and we all can become more well-rounded and holistically prepared individuals when we embrace new experiences and positive influences.

I have seen time and time again extraordinary transformations take place on university campuses. HBCUs are especially fertile with opportunities for new beginnings of all sorts. For many young people, walking onto a university campus marks their first time living away from their families, and the beginning of their independent adult life. When students cross this threshold, they have the chance to reinvent themselves, and to be shaped by the ideas and people they meet in school. It's an amazing and thrilling moment in one's life! Some students come to campus with a complex about their natural hair after being told their entire lives that what grows from their head is unprofessional and ugly. Those same students return home for the holidays wearing proud Afros and embracing their natural beauty after learning self-acceptance in the Black-affirming havens of our institutions.

Others will come to our schools having felt ostracized in their hometown communities because of their unconventional interests or actions. They might be shy students, reserved and reluctant to settle in with the rest of the student body. They may have never known what it was like to fit in and have a sense of belonging before. Our schools are incredibly diverse and filled with people from various backgrounds and fields of interest. These students who were once feeling shy and isolated begin to build community in a way that is authentic and based in true belonging. Like butterflies emerging from their cocoons, they blossom into active leaders on campus. Suddenly they are running for student government or pledging a fraternal organization. Maybe they have lifted their voice in the choir, joined a theater troupe, or tried out for a sports team. They find themselves doing things they never thought they would have the courage or capacity to do.

Others still come to university quite unprepared for what is about to happen to them and all the things they are yet to experience. They may not have had the best test scores, and they may not have the kind of world exposure to prepare them for the diversity of thought and lifestyle they will encounter when they arrive. They also might not have had the important character-building experiences and training they need to be successful in the world just yet. They may have never had anyone to train them in integrity or help them to think critically and form a strong sense of self. These students may not have ever been challenged to develop a strong work ethic or expected to reach outside their comfort zone to achieve new heights. They may not have had encouragement or emotional support from their family, which is a significant indicator in college success. Our schools welcome all these different types of students and offer them what was not readily available to them in the communities where they came from. We offer them the chance to experience new influences, and to transform through life experiences, with support and guidance from a caring community.

For many adults, our formative years are long behind us, and we cannot go backwards to change the things that have happened to us or the choices we've made in the past. However, as long as we are still alive, we can always embrace each opportunity before us to do better, and to evolve. There is always a new experience to be had and lesson to be learned.

Good character is critical to the advancement of our communities and to the next generation, who are the hope for our future. Good character protects us and strengthens us when all else fails and enables us to remain dignified even in undignified situations. When we employ good character, we can rest assured knowing that we are standing for what is right and doing our best to reach our greatest potential as human beings. If we can remain open to positive change with intention and rely on the truth to guide our path, we will surely be headed in the right direction, and well on our way to a bright and powerful future.

CHAPTER 2

VISION

For me, a vision is an extraordinary thought, dream, or idea that has an outcome that enhances, in whole or in part, an individual, group, organization, state, region, or nation. According to my definition, all of us can be visionaries. We can all imagine the great possibilities inherent in that nebulous space between "what is" and "what can be." Your vision does not have to be defined by what other people believe is worthy of pursuit. It can simply be a vision for your career, family, job, business, church, or community. However, having a vision is important because it serves as a guide for where you want to go in life.

Being a visionary means looking inward for confidence, inspiration, and the road map to the future. Visionaries trust in themselves and are moved by the wellspring of excitement that comes from knowing one's purpose. Visionaries draw their own plans and mark their own steps. They don't wait for permission or approval from other people to start making their way toward their goals. Visionaries are people who meet their purpose with courage and set out on their path knowing they will succeed.

Your Vision Matters

Your vision matters, and it matters because it's YOURS. What you see and the way you see it is inherently valuable and unique, because it belongs to you. The way you view the world and the dreams you have inside of you are for you to explore and discover. These are seeds that have been planted within you, and it is your job to feed them, water them, and nurture them into blossoming. Furthermore, what has been placed in you may not be what has been placed in others. This is often the issue for those of us trying to realize our dream, and the thing that ultimately clouds our vision. If you don't act on your vision and live in alignment with the dream in your heart, how will you ever know what change can be brought into the world? Your vision matters, because without it, we all might be stagnant.

The issue of conformity is often a matter of approval and people-pleasing. As I stated in my initial definition, a visionary is someone who looks within for confidence, inspiration, and a plan. Sometimes we look outside of ourselves for approval or for the answers to our questions. We look at what other people are doing and believe that somehow what they have to offer the world is more important than what we are bringing. Even when we have the desire to innovate or try new ideas, fear reshapes that vision into something palatable to others, or one that can easily win approval and be stamped as successful. We become fixated on goals that are not really for us and then wonder why our plans are not working out as well as so-and-so's plans. This is how jealousy and envy creep into our lives and steal our vision. Instead of being focused on ourselves, we focus on others. Instead of dwelling on what we do have and the purpose that God has put in our hearts, we see all the things we lack and all the reasons why we can't fulfill our goals.

Over-valuation of the things that other people do, and not enough emphasis on what we can do ourselves will cataract our vision. This is why it is important to remember that your vision matters. What you are equipped to provide the world is uniquely yours to offer. We must approach vision from a deeply aware sense of self and from a rootedness in who we are. This does not mean that we can't find inspiration in the works of others or involve others in the realization of our dreams. On the contrary, we need to do both things if we are to be successful. However, it is imperative that we maintain sight of the outcomes we desire and not allow what others may say or do determine whether we go after the goals we know we are meant to achieve. If we are grounded in our purpose, we can rest assured that our visions will indeed come to pass.

HBCUs Are Homes for Visionaries

Vision has no color, creed, gender, or income level. Vision can be held by each one of us. However, historically not everyone has been allowed the opportunity to explore their goals, break traditions, or innovate freely. HBCUs are homes for visionaries for this very reason. When the larger American society refused to share resources with Black people in this country, they decided that our ideas and perspectives were not worth investing in, and that our education would not result in meaningful contributions to the world. They were incorrect! Fortunately, a lack of investment or acceptance of Black visionaries was not enough to deter our people from pursuing education, careers, and fulfilling lives. Black visionaries remained steadfast in their purpose and found ways to apply their talent and courage to the goals they wanted to achieve. Because of their resolve, not only were they able to break the mold and be pioneers in new fields, but there was also now a foundation and a foothold for future generations of visionaries to rely on.

The number of visionaries produced by HBCUs is impossible to enumerate, but I have in my mind a few stories that can perfectly illustrate the visionary spirit that is unleashed when our people are equipped with self-confidence, personal drive, and a plan to execute.

Dr. Martin Luther King Jr. and the Civil Rights Movement

Most people are aware of Dr. Martin Luther King Jr. He was an icon in the American Civil Rights Movement, and he has a holiday named in his honor. What many people do not know, however, is that he was a 1948 graduate of HBCU Morehouse College, the only college in the world for African American men. (King's parents were both HBCU alumni as well. His father graduated from Morehouse College, and his mother graduated from Hampton University.) King entered Morehouse, located in his hometown of Atlanta, at the young age of fifteen. During his time there, he was exposed to activists, ministers, and educators who contributed to his intellectual, political, and social development, as well as ideas that helped shape his worldview.

As a minister and copastor of his father's church, Ebenezer

Baptist Church, which at one time was also pastored by his grandfather, King had a front-row seat to his father's philosophy of nonviolence. His Morehouse education combined with his spiritual and religious beliefs transformed King into a leader committed to peace and social justice.

Committed to securing civil rights for all Americans, King led and participated in boycotts, sit-ins, and protests across the South. He also rallied college students to take a stand and support the cause. A sought-after speaker, King spent many nights in jail and was the subject of multiple government investigations because of his leadership role in the Civil Rights Movement.

Imagine the moral vision and courage of Martin Luther King Jr., who stood for human dignity and challenged our nation to move away from centuries of dehumanizing abuses and practices against Blacks. He literally lost his life fighting for the cause that he championed throughout his life.

When I reflect on Dr. King's life and legacy, I am reminded of the exposure HBCUs provide to their students. They introduce them to concepts and ideas associated with their culture and identity in the context of the world in which we live. Many of the people and ideas that shaped Dr. King's life were introduced to him when he was a student at Morehouse College. His vision for a better, more peaceful world was developed, nurtured, and supported by his peers, his teachers, and the school's leaders. That vision, born at an HBCU, changed America and the world!

Ms. Opal Lee and the History of Juneteenth

Another story that illustrates the power of vision is that of Ms. Opal Lee, a Fort Worth, Texas, resident and HBCU graduate.

On June 19th, 1939, at the age of just twelve years old, Ms. Lee witnessed her home violently destroyed by a white mob. Her family had moved into a predominantly white neighborhood, but their presence was deemed a threat by the hostile neighbors. Five hundred rioters lit the family's house aflame, burning all their possessions. This violent crime coincidentally took place on June 19th, a date that would later become Ms. Lee's rallying cry. Today, Ms. Lee's name has become synonymous with Juneteenth, a celebration of emancipation born in Texas and now observed nationally. Ms. Lee worked for federal recognition of Juneteenth for years, but her vision as an educator for the preservation of Black history started long before the holiday was passed into law in 2021.

Ms. Lee was born in 1926 in Marshall, Texas, and throughout her life, she has been working to better her community and uplift African American history. Ms. Lee became a wife and mother before studying at Wiley College, a historically Black institution in Marshall, Texas. She earned a bachelor's degree in elementary education and later a master's in counseling and guidance from North Texas State University. For fifteen years, she served as a passionate educator in the Fort Worth Independent School District in Texas.

After retirement, Ms. Lee dedicated her life to even more civic engagement. She was a founding member of Citizens Concerned with Human Dignity, an organization that works to combat housing inequality. She also volunteered at Habitat for Humanity and served as a board member there. She was a Tarrant County Community Action Agency board member, and an establishing member of the Tarrant County Black Historical and Genealogical Society, an archive dedicated to the research, collection, preservation, and showcasing of African American genealogy and history. Together with the society's founder and fellow four-time HBCU alumna Lenora Rolla, Ms. Lee took on the spirit of the society as a curator, fundraiser, coordinator, promoter, program director, and champion. The stronghold of history is an impressive collection of literature, photos, and artifacts of Black life, and continues to serve as a pillar of African American history and culture through its museum, juried art shows, and historical preservation initiatives.

Ever dedicated to the preservation of African American history, Ms. Lee began her campaign to commemorate Juneteenth at the federal level when she was eighty-nine years old. Her vision was clear—to make Juneteenth a national holiday in her lifetime. For readers who may still be unaware, a full two and a half years after the Emancipation Proclamation was issued, enslaved people in Texas continued toiling at the order of plantation owners despite the federal declaration of freedom in 1865. It wasn't until General Granger and seven thousand colored troops marched to Galveston, Texas, to deliver the news of freedom, as written in General Order No. 3, that enslaved people there knew they were free. The celebration that ensued became memorialized among African Americans as Juneteenth. It is the culmination of a liberatory struggle that marks freedom for all, including the formerly enslaved. While the average American learns July 4th is the day to celebrate sovereignty, our history shows us that a definition of freedom must be defined inclusively for it to truly be considered freedom. It is through the memorialization of Juneteenth that our country can openly reckon with the realities of our past, so that we can truly understand freedom and celebrate it to its fullest.

Unfortunately, until very recently, many Americans of all racial backgrounds were ignorant of this landmark event in American history, and of its importance in our national memory. Ms. Lee believed that Juneteenth ought to be recognized on a national level, and she organized annual 2.5-mile walks, in reference to the two and a half years that those enslaved people were kept in captivity after emancipation. She also planned a symbolic march to Washington in 2016 to plead her case for federal recognition of Juneteenth to former president Barack Obama. (She did not end up meeting then with President Obama, though she met him later.) Ms. Lee's march gathered hundreds of walkers and over 1.6 million signatures of an online petition to make Juneteenth a permanent fixture of our national calendar. Her dream ignited a historical movement for freedom and inclusion nationwide.

What I find most inspiring about Ms. Lee's dedication to Juneteenth is her steadfast vision not only for African Americans but for American history.

"Juneteenth is not a Texas thing. It's not a Black thing. We're talking about freedom, for everyone," Ms. Lee said during her visit to the White House in 2021.

On June 17th, 2021, President Joe Biden finally signed the Juneteenth National Independence Day Act into law. Ms. Lee was present for the signing of the law, where her vision for the preservation of African American history was cemented into the memory of our nation's legal calendar.

Ms. Lee was nominated for a Nobel Peace Prize in 2022 for

her civil rights work, a nomination justly marking the legacy of this powerful pioneer for change. I most admire the way that she works diligently for her community, and how through each season of her life she has found a way to contribute even more of herself to her people and her nation. At ninety-six years old, Ms. Opal is the epitome of a visionary. She continues to bring her great ideas and dreams to fruition, and her efforts are invariably to the benefit of everyone around her.

The vision statement of Wiley College is to serve as "a beacon of light inspiring individuals to serve as catalysts of social change in their community and professions." When I consider the vision of this great institution, and the contributions of Ms. Lee's long life and legacy, I can confidently say that Wiley's mission has indeed been fulfilled through Ms. Opal Lee.

Jonathan Quarles and the Flint Water Crisis

Another great visionary whose story I have learned of is a young entrepreneur named Jonathan Quarles. Mr. Quarles' mission to address great issues of public health in his native Flint, Michigan, illustrates the powerful intersection of innovation and environmental justice. Mr. Quarles is the founder of Quartz Water Source, and his vision was to help his community while building a business in the process. In 2014, when the Flint water crisis began, headlines exploded with the news that an entire city's water had been compromised, with dangerous and potentially deadly results. In that moment, we all learned what residents of Flint had known for some time—their water contained extremely elevated levels of lead. The contaminated water was pervasive—public institutions like schools and official buildings, private businesses, and over 40 percent of homes were found to be affected by the poisonous water being pumped through the city. Furthermore, it was found that a gross neglect of the public was being carried out by local politicians to cover up the problem and dismiss cases filed by citizens. The negligence resulted in a series of choices from official leaders that willfully put the health of Flint residents at risk.

Access to clean water is not an American problem alone. One in three people on the planet lacks adequate access to potable water. For decades now, scientists and engineers have been discussing at length the issue of our world's water sources, and the pollution that certain industries and government protocols allow to the detriment of our global public health. Many solutions have been posited and tested, and the people leading these innovations are some of the true visionaries of our lifetime.

Mr. Quarles, a graduate of HBCU Florida Agricultural and Mechanical University (FAMU), became a global citizen during his time at FAMU, where he lived in a scholarship house full of international students and was encouraged by his roommate to study abroad in South Africa. There he learned about the value of international connections in cultural and political processes. He determined from that moment to be engaged in global travel and study, and it is through his international experiences that his innovative solutions to Flint's water crisis were born.

After traveling to Israel to learn about the cutting-edge water solutions in use there, he became involved in the development of "second line" clean water that could be an additional source for municipal water supplies. The atmospheric water generation technology that he encountered provided a powerful alternative solution to the water crisis by generating clean water from the air. Quarles launched Quartz Water Source in 2019, effectively realizing his vision to marry technological innovation with solution-oriented initiatives for our communities. Today, Mr. Quarles is an entrepreneur, investor, and author. His company was able to secure funding, and despite setbacks due to the coronavirus pandemic, now produces potable water for residents of Flint and Detroit.

The process of applying confidence and inspiration to develop a plan and execute one's vision is one that requires awareness. Visionaries must be aware of the needs around them, and have an awareness of their own capacity to meet those needs. They must also be daring enough to develop a plan, and to launch it at the right time, despite whatever unforeseen obstacles may abound. Visionaries are aware of something that I think everyone ought to consider, which is that though we hope some authority would come to fix the world, to rectify the problems and create the solutions, we everyday humans are also imbued with the power, and with the influence, intelligence, and resources, to create change. Sometimes, all it takes is a little gumption.

How to Be Daring

Being daring is a practice. You don't wake up daring—most of us don't, anyway. It's not always so simple as getting out of bed ready to take on the world. Like anything else, a daring attitude can be cultivated, and it comes from the development of that visionary spirit—the ability to look inward for confidence, inspiration, and a plan. I encourage having a plan, but I don't believe you need a plan to start developing a daring attitude. Sometimes we don't know what's coming around the corner, but we've got to at least have enough nerve to take the next step. If you start with confidence and inspiration, life will guide you to your purpose, and you will begin pulling the pieces of your puzzle together.

When it comes to developing a sense of confidence, it's important to remember that who you are and what you have to offer the world matters. It is relevant to your community, and it is why you are here. Self-confidence comes from deciding this and being sure about it. This is not to say that things won't arise that might knock you off your square, or that you won't need to be occasionally humbled to gain some new perspective. Through every experience that you have, remember that you are in the driver's seat of your own life. You oversee how you get to feel about yourself, and you can choose to see the best in yourself, and to move forward believing that what you have to offer is good. Practicing this looks different for different people. Maybe you develop a mantra that reminds you of who you are and the values you hold. Perhaps you spend time in meditation and prayer to help ground you and quiet negative voices and doubts.

It is also important to practice taking risks and putting yourself out there. Oftentimes it is a fear of failure or looking stupid that holds us back from trying new things. Developing confidence is also about developing a resistance to the fear of failure. Failure is a given; mistakes are an essential part of the process in any visionary's journey to success. If you dare to fail, you also dare to succeed, and in small ways you can challenge yourself to try new things and navigate new experiences that might be uncomfortable or hard to manage. While some folks say that you must leave your comfort zone to grow, I like to think of comfort zones as spaces that expand with every new experience. Where you once had only a small sphere of confidence, each time you stretch yourself, you become more assured and more comfortable in your ability to gracefully navigate new situations. As you gain new tools, and a newfound familiarity, your comfort zone grows with you, and you can establish even more self-confidence in a broader range of contexts and circumstances.

Ultimately, each person must determine a way to develop that sense of inner trust and resolve. Be diligent in maintaining this attitude, for it will serve you well on your journey to fulfill your purpose.

Developing inner inspiration is about finding the inspiration that resonates with you. It's not about being self-absorbed and only invested in your own ideas. It is more about developing the ability to be moved to action by the ideas that you encounter. For example, Ms. Opal, in her dedication to values of service and education, was inspired by the work of civic engagement around her. She joined in initiatives that resonated with her own convictions, and this ignited her inner sense of inspiration. Likewise, Mr. Quarles' personal desire to be internationally connected through innovations and solutions led him to meet and collaborate with the people who could share with him the information and technology he needed. External inspiration from others is a beginning. It is when we are internally changed by what we experience, learn, and study that a sense of internal inspiration is fed and sustained. As you develop your visionary spirit, consider the inspirations that resonate within you. What are your values, goals, ambitions, and desires? What are the stories that have encouraged you, given you hope and an overwhelming sense of possibility and adventure? These are the things that will guide you to your plan and ultimately inform the choices you make in life.

While you will undoubtedly draw inspiration from others to sustain it within yourself, it's important to remember that your vision is your own. It is your road and your map. Sometimes we think that if we share our vision with other people, then they can affirm our choices and we can feel more confident in our ability and our plan. This is not always so. Sometimes we do need help, but oftentimes when we lack self-confidence and inspiration, trying to plan with the help of others turns out to be to our detriment. It is important to trust in your own true north, and believe that if you maintain your vision, you will arrive at your destination with all that you need to be successful. Visionaries are so important for our world because they can chart paths and realize ideas that no one else has been able to do before. You have not been granted sight simply to watch others. You have been granted a vision because someone must lead the way to new ideas, places, and ways of being. Others may not see what you see, and this can be discouraging. What you see is still important, and once you clarify your plan, and mobilize toward its completion, the work you do will speak for and represent itself. Trust that you are capable, move when you are inspired, and march toward the future you dream of. You are a visionary, and the world is ready and waiting for your contributions.

CHAPTER 3

WORK ETHIC

A work ethic is a dedicated practice and standard for one's personal work. I believe that there really is no substitute for hard work, and that few tools are more useful than a reliable standard for quality self-assessment. While there are certainly circumstances outside of our control that contribute to our success and achievements, I've always found that the harder I worked, the luckier I got. I think this is still true today, despite a lot of recent changes to the work world and the way that we as a modern society relate to work. Working consistently and having a definitive standard for one's work is essential to an empowered work ethic.

A work ethic, like character, is shaped by influences, but it can also be cultivated and crafted. A work ethic is a marriage of character and skill—it requires that we consider the tasks before us and approach them with a sense of value and dignity. My mother and father were extremely hard-working individuals, and they taught with words around the dinner table and by example with their actions. One of my favorite and most memorable experiences learning about a work ethic involves the time my father trained me for my first-ever entrepreneurial endeavor.

At the age of nine, I became fascinated by an advertisement in a magazine. I am uncertain of the publication's exact title, but I believe it was called *Boys Life*, and within the advertisement was the opportunity for young readers to begin a money-making endeavor. The idea was to purchase fifty fancy eight-by-ten wall placards designed with memorable Bible verses, resell them at a higher value, and earn a bit of profit. I think the purchase price was fifty cents each and they were to be sold for one dollar. A successful sale of all stock would mean a twenty-five dollar profit, which was quite a sum for a nine-year-old boy in 1950.

My father approved of this venture and agreed to front me a loan—I didn't have the start-up cash I needed to purchase my first order of products. Before I could get approved for Daddy's loan, I had to learn a few lessons to prepare for the job. I was getting ready for door-to-door sales and would need quite a bit of customer service training. My father taught me how to dress and the importance of making eye contact when speaking to people. He told me what to emphasize about my business, quizzed me on knowledge of the Bible verses on the placards I was selling, and gave general advice on how to approach a homeowner.

Finally, I was ready for my first test run. I went outside our house and rang the doorbell.

"Hello, young man. What can I do for you?" Daddy said.

With one hand in my pocket and the other gripping a fistful of sheets, I started grinning, fidgeting, and fumbling my sales pitch. Daddy slammed the door right in my face. Confused, I rang the doorbell once more.

"Hello, young man. What can I do for you?" Daddy repeated.

"Why did you shut the door in my face?" I asked.

"Because you did not act like you were serious about what you were selling," he replied.

From there he continued my training, and together we went over how I should explain what I was selling, and why I thought homeowners should buy my goods. He also taught me to stand up straight and get some control over my nervous fidgets and grinning. Daddy's objective was to emphasize a knowledge of my business, eye contact, good presentation, confidence in telling my story, and good money practices in conducting the financial transaction. I wasn't to take credit or partial payments.

After this second round of training, I went back to the doorbell for another trial run. After preparation and reassurance, I nailed my pitch.

"I think you're ready," Daddy said. I was approved for my small business loan.

After selling the first batch, I continued my business and sold a total of five orders of fifty placards. About twenty-five years later, I was reminded of my first money-making operation when, on a visit to the home of an elderly woman, I saw there hanging up on her wall one of my Bible verse placards still on display.

Building Strong Habits

The lessons my father taught me during those days of training for my first foray into work laid the foundation for my work habits and the defining pillars of my work ethic. Those pillars are Preparation, Poise, Consistency, and Risk.

PREPARATION

Preparation is multilayered, and it's the first pillar of a work ethic. To become proficient at any given task, we need to learn what it takes to be successful and then set ourselves up for success every time. When I first rang the doorbell of my parents' home that day to practice my skills, I was superficially prepared. I had on the right clothes, and I had all my materials. I was in the right place, and I was seemingly ready to do what I set out to do, which was to make some money. However, once pressed for more information about what I was selling, it was clear that I was not fully prepared for the task before me. I didn't have the right body language and physical demeanor. I wasn't putting my time to good use, and I had not calculated the kind of pressure I would feel in a real-life marketing situation.

I couldn't know how I would react to the pressure until I had a real experience under it. We are all on a learning journey, and some things we cannot predict or prepare for in advance. Yet it is preparation that makes all the difference when uncertainty and confusion arise. When the unpredictable happens, and for the challenges that you can't see coming, preparation is priceless. When you're committed to good time management and are already practicing good habits, those unexpected curveballs from life won't throw you for a loop in the same way.

Sometimes we think we are prepared because we look the part, or because we've ticked off the boxes for what we're "supposed" to do. We've got the degree, we've had the internship, and we might even have a few lines on our resume. These are certainly great first steps, but a strong work ethic is not about ticking boxes and being just good enough to get by. A work ethic is about having a standard, having a personal expectation of quality in everything that we do. A lot of young students who enter a university come from places where they are big fish in small ponds. They are naturally talented and don't have to push themselves to meet the standards of their high school courses. When they get to college, they've got to prove themselves in a new pond, where there are bigger fish, and even bigger distractions lurk in the waters. The amount of preparation needed to meet the same benchmarks of achievement has increased significantly, and some students are not ready for such a steep performance curve. Furthermore, once you leave the world of higher education, those benchmarks of success are not as outwardly impressive. Job interviewers are not going to ask you about your GPA or what academic organization you were elected to lead. You've got to build your own benchmarks, based on where you want to go in life.

As I touched upon in the previous chapter, I believe that if you are to be truly self-empowered, your personal convictions, your vision, and your terms of success must be created by you, and not by external sources. Your goals are set by you, and your preparation will determine whether and how you reach those goals. The world of work has changed immensely since I first entered it in 1950. There are more options and industries, new technologies and fields of study. Despite all that diversity of choice, it is still a personal standard of preparation that will set you apart and make you the best you can be. Whatever your aspirations, remember that this is not about looking the part and being passable in someone else's valuation of success. It is about mapping a plan for your own future as defined by you.

Preparation means taking the time to practice the things that you're unsure of and getting advice and input where you may lack understanding. It means making every effort to be on time for your appointments, and to come ready to learn from every interaction and experience you are lucky enough to get. Preparation also often requires a shift in priorities and perspective. Do you know what you need, and do you know how to have it consistently? Figure out the preparation equation that you need for your success. If you need to get an A in your 8 a.m. biology course to keep your 3.0 average and scholarship, how many hours of sleep do you realistically need to get if you are to be up and ready for class by 7 a.m.? There are some important calculations we must make if we want to be prepared. This lesson is not just for bleary-eyed coeds who made the rookie mistake of registering for 8 a.m. classes. At every moment in your life, you've got to plan your daily activities around your goals and set yourself up for success.

You risk falling behind your own talent when you lack preparation. Some of the most creative, intelligent, and innovative minds miss opportunities to realize their potential due to lack of preparation. The funny thing is that preparation is the bare minimum you can do to ensure success, and the main factor of good preparation is time management. Giving yourself enough time to be attentive and deliberate will help you prepare for each level of advancement in your life and career. The eager nine-year-old that I was, I bounded confidently to the front door, hasty to prove myself to my father. I could have been discouraged when Daddy said I wasn't ready, but the truth is that I needed more time to really be equipped for my new job. Give yourself the head start to your success by planning well with your time, and don't be discouraged if you need more time to be prepared. The race that you are running is against yourself, and the person who gains the most from your good work ethic is you. Doing your best and doing what you must to be truly prepared will always be worth your while.

CONSISTENCY

Consistency is key. I know you've heard it before. This phrase is, as they say, "played out." I'd like to add a word to the phrase and say that consistency is the skeleton key—it opens most doors you want to walk through.

The same way that preparation requires a dedication of time, so does consistency. Consistency is about repetition, drilling, and hammering in the skills we need to always have on hand. Whether learning a new language, sport, piece of music, or steps to a dance, it is repeated practice that helps us cement what we know into our work ethic. Think about your job or profession right now. What are the things that you need to know like the back of your hand to be successful? What are the things you do every day without even thinking? You don't have to think about them, because you do them so regularly that they no longer require that much effort from you to accomplish. Let's not confuse the ease with which you do these tasks with simplicity. You might be an engineer doing highly technical repair work, or an analyst dealing in intricate patterns and equations. The tasks themselves have not gotten any less difficult to master, but you have mastered them with time and repetition. No matter the task, a continual effort to practice and improve will always unlock new levels of success.

It's important to be consistent for yourself more than anyone else. Being consistent allows you to prove your abilities to yourself first and prove that you can accomplish something over and over again. Just as preparation offers perspective, consistency develops confidence and self-trust. Being consistent shows your dedication to your work, and the standards that you set forth for yourself.

Being consistent is also a way to show other people who you are and to build your reputation. This is another reason why I believe that consistency is the skeleton key. Your reputation is important! Your reputation is not only what people see on the outside, but what they know of your work. When you have high standards for your work, people notice. People want hard workers on their team. They want people who can demonstrate preparedness and poise in difficult situations, and they want teammates who exhibit strong character and integrity. When people want to help you, to do you a favor, offer you a leg up, or put in a good word for you to aid in your advancement, they want to know that you can reliably produce all these things. Your reputation is often a reflection of your work ethic, and a good reputation is one that has been proven to be true over time.

When I think of the value of consistency, I also think about some experiences that HBCU students have in many of our top-performing business schools. As students are being prepared for future careers in entrepreneurship, finance, and all aspects of business, they must learn first and foremost how to present themselves. First-year business courses are usually large, and at any time that a student raises their voice to speak, they are trained to formally introduce themselves. They say their name, their course of study, and the place they come from. Each time! Students are taught to project their voice, make eye contact, and speak clearly. Business students must adhere to business dress codes on specific days during the week and learn to exhibit an appearance appropriate for the professional field they will likely enter in a few years' time. They are also sometimes put on the spot, made to discuss current events and topics of national or international interest, as a test of their ability to think on their feet and maintain confidence under pressure. It can be a little nerve-racking to introduce yourself to large groups of people repeatedly. Sometimes there are important people in the room with these students—visiting speakers, entrepreneurs, and recruiters, people who have influence and whose respect they hope to gain. What many students don't realize during the process is that they are being prepared with a gold standard. When the time comes, they will be ready to present themselves, and their impressive reputations will already be loading.

At Hampton, we teach our students to exemplify the characteristics of what we refer to as the "Hampton Man" and "Hampton Woman." These qualities include good character and excellent behavior. The Hampton Man and Hampton Woman carry and present themselves in a respectful and professional manner, representing themselves, their families, and the university well at all times and in all settings. Visitors to our campus are always impressed with our students' preparedness and poise.

POISE

I believe that having self-assurance and maintaining composure is an important part of a work ethic, because the way that we regulate our emotional responses or employ wisdom in difficult situations can have positive or negative effects on the quality and effectiveness of our work. Maintaining composure and self-control in today's age seems to be a lost art. When I see what our politicians and elected officials permit themselves to say and do on social media, I become more than a little concerned for our world and the young people coming of age in it. I think that being poised is an empowering quality for young people to have in a world where everyone's self-control is being chipped at every minute through notifications, incendiary headlines, and social-media attention traps. Your ability to manage yourself, to maintain composure, and to keep a level head will serve you greatly wherever you go—in the workplace, at home, and out in the public sphere.

What I have also learned throughout my life is that the more committed I am to a practice of preparation, the more poise and composure I have in uncomfortable or high-pressure situations. Some folks may have a naturally winning poker face, but most of us must put in some work to get good at regulating our responses under pressure. I believe that preparation correlates so strongly with poise because preparation grants perspective. When you have been working hard, focusing on your goals, and training for your aspirations continually, you gain a self-confidence that no one can take away, and you gain an understanding of what it takes to meet a standard of excellence that isn't mysterious or unattainable. So, when difficult circumstances arise, when there is high pressure to perform and critical stakes on the line, you know what to do. You can see what's most important in a situation, and you are equipped with the perspective necessary to make the right move forward.

Maintaining composure also has powerful benefits for our society, in ways that I feel have been greatly undervalued in our current day. Being poised and composed is not just about respectability, and maintaining one's composure doesn't mean remaining silent in unfair situations or taking all emotionality out of the workplace. Our passions, convictions, and opinions are a relevant part of our work, and it would not be to our benefit to extract these things from the contributions we make in the workplace. However, we must all learn how to communicate our opinions and needs with respect for ourselves and for the people around us.

I am reminded of a young HBCU graduate who we'll call Amber. Amber currently works for a premier digital-tech company based in the United States. When she first started, Amber was struggling to enjoy her experience at work. The team she was working on just wasn't the best fit for her talents and goals, and she questioned whether she could remain at the company.

"People didn't like that I was a Black girl with my head held high, and they did everything in their power to snuff it out," Amber recalled.

Despite this, Amber continued to work hard, as she had been trained to do. She was consistent and prepared, and she outperformed her peers. She also joined the network of Black employees in the company, an informal group that provided support and community in their corporate environment. She became known for her work ethic and a sense of pride that enabled her to be a strong self-advocate when issues came up in the workplace.

In the summer of 2020, during the height of the first coronavirus wave and one of the most poignant reckonings of police violence in our nation, Amber became suddenly drawn into a leadership role in diversity, equity, and inclusion talks with top executives in her company. In light of protests and international conversations about racial equity, Amber found herself in a position to make a difference. The diversity, equity, and inclusion department at her company was not prepared to answer questions and provide insight in the same way that she was able to do so, having been prepared and trained at an HBCU.

"Even though it's not my job to educate, if I have a listening ear for someone who has access to resources and can affect change, it is my responsibility as a Black person and HBCU alumna," said Amber.

In the high pressure of a global pandemic and an outcry for more diversity in corporate spaces, Amber was poised to rise to the challenge. She had been working hard at her job, and she had also been trained for this very moment through her HBCU experience to speak up and be a voice for change. Racial conversations in this country continue to be contentious, and with high visibility comes the risk of backlash. When emotions run high, it's easy to say things you might regret, to lose your cool or become discouraged and fatalistic about situations that are hard to navigate. Yet, Amber remained poised and prepared, knowing that this opportunity would be one to stand out and offer useful guidance and information to her colleagues. Today, the CEO of her company knows exactly who she is, and some of the initiatives she helped design for inclusion have been seriously adopted into the company's work.

"I saw it as a chance to advance my career, and my HBCU experience gave me the confidence so that I felt like I didn't have to prove anything to anyone," said Amber.

"I'm proud of the way that I was able to get what I wanted out of it and to also make the world a better place."

RISK

A healthy work ethic will also push you forward toward risk, as well as rewards. Risk is the possibility of suffering a harm or loss, and it is something we all must contend with as we strive to be the best at what we do. It's easy to become risk averse at certain points in our lives and careers. We've worked hard to get to where we are, and we don't want to jeopardize what we've already worked for by making choices with uncertain or potentially dangerous outcomes. Put simply, we are afraid of loss or failure.

Two of the most poignant and thoughtful reflections about navigating risk and failure come from the great mind of HBCU graduate Oprah Winfrey. Oprah attended Tennessee State University, where she studied communications before launching her pioneering career in television, film, and journalism. You already know who she is! Oprah's words can serve as encouragement for everyone to see how a strong work ethic is reinforced by an ability to be open to risk, and to accept failure as a teacher of success.

"I believe that one of life's greatest risks is never daring to risk," Oprah once said. "Do the one thing you think you cannot do. Fail at it. Try again. Do better the second time."

When we are too afraid to take risks, we chance missing out on opportunities to grow, to refine our skills, and ultimately to succeed. "Fail at it," Oprah says. Whatever it is that you want to do, fail at it first, because failure will not have the last word. The recipe for improvement will always be this: Fail, try again, do better.

When we take risks, we refine our work ethic and gain new tools in the process. Failure provides us with new information, perspective, and wisdom that we otherwise would not have gained without first making attempts at our goals.

Another Oprah Winfrey quote that offers a powerful perspective is from her 2013 address to the graduating class at Harvard University. In her speech, she shared about the initial failures she experienced launching her OWN network after twenty-five years of number one ratings of *The Oprah Winfrey Show* on a major network. Amid frustration, embarrassment, and pressure, Oprah realized a few things about failure and hard work.

"It doesn't matter how far you might rise, at some point you are bound to stumble," she said. "Because if you're constantly doing what we do, raising the bar, if you are constantly pushing yourself higher and higher, the law of averages, not to mention the myth of Icarus, predicts that you will at some point fall. When you do, I want you to know this—remember this: There is no such thing as failure. Failure is just life trying to move us in another direction."

This refreshing perspective on failure offers a lot of grace to those still figuring out their way through life, and let me tell you, that's all of us. If, after a twenty-five-year career of unde-niable and unbeatable success, Oprah Winfrey could still feel humbled by missing the mark, then none of us are immune to the challenges of risk and failure. What I have learned is that risk offers us the chance to prove that in addition to preparation, poise, and consistency, our standards for excellence also produce a relentless pursuit to push past obstacles and learn continu-ously about life and ourselves.

Imposter Syndrome

Unfortunately, many people in today's society believe that fi-nances, grades, awards, and the like are entitlements and should be given and not earned. This causes immeasurable harm to our young people, and to the industries in which they will one day be the leaders. We need hard-working and confident individuals at the helm of our society. When you skip past hard work and go straight to reward, you miss a huge part of the journey that makes your experiences meaningful. What I see as the problem with entitlement is that it robs you of your talent, work ethic, in-tegrity, and, ultimately, your dignity. An entitlement mindset will turn a talented person into a mediocre one. This kind of attitude will also shave away at a person's work ethic, and make them less prepared, poised, consistent, and daring. A corrosion of stan-dards leads to less integrity, and a diminished sense of dignity.

I've recently heard of a phenomenon called "imposter syn-drome" that sometimes plagues young professionals, and even folks more established in their careers. From what I understand, and what *Psychology Today* has to say about it, imposter syndrome is a condition where people believe they are undeserving of their achievements and the high esteem in which they are generally held. They struggle with perfectionism, fear of success, and self-effacement. Unfortunately, feeling like you don't deserve the achievements you have will have significant impacts on your life and career.

This kind of self-doubt and self-sabotage will compromise your ability to do meaningful work. I think there is a thin line between expecting the best from ourselves and a crippling sense of perfectionism. We should strive to do our best, but we should also be able to accept mistakes and failures as a healthy part of our development and journeys as people.

Luckily, imposter syndrome is not a fatal condition, and the main side effects of perfectionism, fear of success, and lack of self-effacement can be abetted through a change of perspective about our abilities.

I believe there may be some links between imposter syndrome and what many people in the Black community might call the "Twice as Good" motto. It has been cemented in our culture that for Black people to achieve just half of the status and position as their white counterparts, they must be twice as good as their peers. Also known as "The Black Tax," there persists a notion that Black people must outperform and overperform to receive a modicum of what is handed to others, and I fear that this kind of mindset is harmful to our children, young people, and all the rest of us, too.

The late comedian, activist, and author Dick Gregory rejected such a notion and did not believe that children should have such expectations put on them so early in life.

"Don't teach your children that they have to be twice as good," he once said in an interview. "That's an awful thing to teach a child. That's like saying because you're Black, white America has a right to change your dollar for ninety-four cents."

I think imposter syndrome in Black communities can be fueled by this notion that our work is not equal to the work of others, and that we don't deserve to be valued in the same ways that our counterparts are because of our race. It teaches us to be ashamed of who we are, and to feel that we must overcompensate to make up for what we are lacking in the eyes of the powers that be. It robs us of our own sense of dignity to place an unfair standard of work on ourselves for the sake of appealing to those in power.

Instead, we ought to herald standards that enable us to find dignity and self-assurance in all situations. In one of his final speeches before his assassination, Martin Luther King Jr. stood before a group of striking sanitation workers in Memphis, Tennessee, rousing support for the Poor People's Campaign. The workers had been on strike for over a month, fighting for equitable wages. In his speech, MLK delivers a piece of wisdom that I think can be useful to all of us involved in labor.

"Whenever you are engaged in work that serves humanity and is for the building of humanity, it has dignity, and it has worth," said Dr. King.

This speech was meant to build solidarity among workers across class lines, and to remind them of the dignity that comes from the work ethic and service that they contribute as human beings. We ought to be able to draw a sense of dignity from our work. This dignity is what I would suggest using to combat the doubting, perfectionism, and anxiety of imposter syndrome.

Instead of worrying about who we aren't in the eyes of others, we should rest on what we know about our work ethic and find peace in the things that we have been able to accomplish despite the obstacles and challenges along the way. I know that while HBCUs can sometimes house elitist ideas of perfectionism that perpetuate the "Twice as Good" mentality, the concept must persist in other schools as well. I also believe that a work ethic can be cultivated by anyone, anywhere, and so can a sense of dignity and pride in one's own contributions to the world. For those reading this book and seeking support in the struggle for a strong work ethic, I suggest that you find yourself in community with others looking for the same thing. Continue to build up your personal standards, your preparation, your consistency, your poise, and your boldness, but also find those who exemplify these things and come together around what it means to be dignified in work. Just imagine what a group of people with a strong work ethic and an empowered sense of self can accomplish together.

CHAPTER 4

SERVICE

In 2017, former NASA mathematician and HBCU graduate Katherine Johnson graced Hampton University's commencement with a heartfelt message for our graduating class. In her speech, she spoke of the honor of a Hampton education, and the importance of doing one's best in all that one endeavors to do. She also encouraged students to employ service in their lives, noting the value that it brings, not only to those who receive help, but to those performing the service as well.

"Go as many places as you can, to help as many persons as you can," she said. "Make it worth their while, and it'll be worth your while all your life to know that you helped."

For me, service is truly an exhilarating experience. To realize how one's own efforts might influence the less fortunate is exciting, inspirational, and gratifying. It is also essential to the advancement and maintenance of our society, and a wellspring of opportunity for those who know how to seize it.

Help, support, or service can be demonstrated in a number

of different ways. One can donate time, money, or clothes, or care for a sick family member, friend, loved one, or stranger. One can also volunteer as a leader or mentor with an organization or serve as a coach, tutor, or advocate. It doesn't matter in what capacity you serve, only that you develop a mindset to be of service to others whenever possible.

Some may say that their financial, educational, and social status prevent them from being of service to others. This is not so. Dr. Martin Luther King Jr., a proud Morehouse graduate, once said, "Everybody can be great because anybody can serve. You don't have to have a college degree to serve. You only need a heart full of grace. A soul generated by love."

The reality is that we often do not make the time for service or elevate service as a priority in our lives. In our search to build strong careers and advance in our own projects, we become singularly focused on our own advancement, and we forget the value and virtue of lifting others up or considering the needs of others before our own. Of course, there are some seasons of our lives that demand more personal investment, and we cannot give to others from an empty cup. However, service is a virtue of community, and when that virtue is lost, it is the entire community that feels the burden. Likewise, through service, our lives draw great meaning, and in meeting the needs of others, we come to fortify ourselves as well.

The Personal and Professional Benefits of Service

We often like to think of service as an action meant to be purely altruistic and entirely in the interest of those receiving help. Indeed, service is principally about giving of oneself for the benefit of others, and I do believe that this should be the first reason why one's spirit is led to serve. However, it is equally true that when one gives of oneself, he or she will also always receive. Consider the universal adage that "you reap what you sow." If one sows service, he or she will indeed reap the benefits of that service in some way. It is not entirely wrong for young people to approach serving others with the thought in mind that they might also have something to gain. For there are many things to be gained through service, and many things that we would not have today were it not for the selfless works of others.

The exchange of values that occurs when one becomes involved in group service activities and projects can be invaluable to a person in search of both community and guidance. While wisdom can be conferred through words, speeches, books, and theoretical ideas, it is only through application and real-life experiences that we can integrate what we have learned. Service is one such way that we can apply our theoretical knowledge and beliefs to the real world, and leaders and change-makers are often using this particular method to reinforce their goals and beliefs. To put it another way, engagement in community service can offer the opportunity to acquire knowledge and experience that otherwise would not be accessible. In service, you may also encounter other people who embody the traits and characteristics that you hope to attain. You can build community and demonstrate your talents in a way that benefits others. In addition, you may be exposed to new places, people, and realities that you may never have encountered before.

Consider the experiences of a former HBCU student named Chelsea during her time as a participant and leader of an alternative spring break program. Alternative spring break programs are popular programs at certain universities that organize service trips for students as an alternative to the more common spring break activities that include traveling and partying. Through alternative spring break programs, students are still able to travel, but instead they do so for the purpose of putting their hands to work in a project for others. These projects range from disaster relief to community outreach to high-school tutoring and support.

For Chelsea, her alternative break experience involved providing educational support for underperforming youth in an inner-city school. Each day, her group of college undergrads would visit the school site and participate in sessions with their high school counterparts. Chelsea worked with one student in particular, a young man who was actually about her age but was still working through his high-school coursework. Together they worked to finish the lessons set forth by his school's program.

While practicing math questions, Chelsea noticed that her student was exceptionally good at quick mental math. He was sharp and accurate, and she wondered how a bright young man with clear academic talent could find himself so behind in his schoolwork. She also noticed that his cell phone was continually ringing and vibrating with texts and notifications, which she thought was interesting, and a little disruptive. Ultimately, Chelsea felt concern for her student, whose situation to her was so clearly a product of under-resourced education and inner-city educational failings. She resolved to bring up this observation during their leader debrief meeting at the end of the service day.

When she recounted her experience working with the popular

and quick-minded young man, Chelsea lamented the injustice of his educational situation. When she finished telling her story, the other members of the group laughed!

"Girl, you know he's probably a drug dealer," they said. Her friends explained to her that it was likely the young man was good at calculations because he was constantly making transactions and handling money, and that the calls and messages to his phone were probably orders and directions for his hustle.

Until that moment, Chelsea had not once considered this possibility in her interactions with the young student. She noticed his ability and skill in calculation and the activity on his phone, but she had not stopped to look closely at the individual before her, and the realities that might be informing his particular set of academic strengths and struggles. She had drawn from stereotypes to paint a picture of his circumstances, but when she reconsidered, she recognized that she did not know much about him really. She didn't know anything about his home life or his childhood, or the experiences that had brought him to this point where their paths were suddenly converging.

Chelsea laughed *at herself* when she realized that her naivete and quickness to draw conclusions without deeper inquiry had stopped her from being able to see the young man in his full experience, whatever it may have been.

Today, Chelsea is several years into her career as a criminal defense lawyer, and she cites this interesting moment of reflection as a changing point in her thought processes about people. It made her more aware, and prompted her to consider people's circumstances and how their situations impact the way that they show up in the world. In exposing her own ignorance, and revealing the limitations of her own experience, this time of service enabled her to grow professionally. As a lawyer handling cases for people going through what may be the most difficult and trying moments of their lives, she has learned that asking questions, probing, and being curious and thorough are essential skills for success in her field. She cannot rest on her own assumptions or allow her mind to fill in details based on stereotypes and preconceived ideas. She must always seek greater understanding to offer each of her clients fair and unbiased representation. What Chelsea learned through a short experience during a weeklong service trip now stands as an informative moment in her development as an attorney.

The Cornerstone of an HBCU Education

Many of our nation's HBCUs were founded on principles of service and meeting communal needs. Following the Civil War and the emancipation of enslaved Africans in 1865, many HBCUs were chartered in response to the racist barriers that kept Black people from higher education in both public and private schools. Black folks needed formal training to be productive members of society and to build their own communities. Those institutions founded particularly to serve Black people had the herculean task of educating an already poor and underprivileged population with very little in hand, compared to their white counterparts. Over one hundred and fifty years later, HBCUs continue to uphold this same purpose.

The Thurgood Marshall College Fund notes 50 percent of the student body at HBCUs and predominantly Black institutions (PBIs) are low-income or first-generation students. In a nation where higher education is a multibillion-dollar industry and universities with the largest endowments receive the most notoriety and acclaim, providing quality instruction and skills to low-income students is a form of service that cannot be overlooked. No other institutions produce as many professionals or offer as much support and upward mobility to marginalized communities as HBCUs. I believe a strong commitment to service and to the strengthening of our communities is central to what sets our historically Black institutions apart and in a class of their own.

The Hampton University alma mater contains the lyrics, "O Hampton, we never can make thee a song, except as our lives do the singing. In service that will thy great spirit prolong and send it through centuries ringing!" These beautiful lines remind me that service is indeed a sweet song, and that the impacts of work undertaken for the collective really do echo out through generations.

Activism and Service

It would be nearly impossible to name all the activists and change-makers who received their educations from historically Black institutions. For quite the same reason that our institutions tend to serve the more marginalized and underrepresented populations of our nation, they have also been strongholds for activism, and important channels for leadership and change.

The Reverend Dr. Martin Luther King Jr. is one of the finest examples of HBCU-bred activism. During his time at Morehouse and throughout his career, Dr. King activated relationships between student organizations at institutions around the nation and the world through his involvement in the Student

Nonviolent Coordinating Committee. Some of the other notable activists who came out of HBCUs include:

Stokely Carmichael, a graduate of Howard University

Ella Baker, a graduate of Shaw University

W. E. B. Du Bois, founder of the NAACP and graduate of Fisk University

Booker T. Washington, a graduate of Hampton University and founder of the Tuskegee Institute

Thurgood Marshall, a graduate of Lincoln University and Howard University

Alice Walker, a graduate of Spelman College, former professor at Jackson State University and Tougaloo College

John Lewis, a graduate of Fisk University, chairman of the Student Nonviolent Coordinating Committee

Jesse Jackson, a graduate of North Carolina A&T University

These are just a few household names who have fought for justice, advancement, and the liberation of Black people. What is not so openly known or spoken about today is the fact that HBCUs also provide education for leaders and activists of the African diaspora and have historically provided significant support in the colonial liberation struggles of several African nations. The first president of Nigeria was a graduate of Lincoln University and a classmate of both the prolific poet Langston Hughes and Thurgood Marshall, the first African American United States Supreme Court justice. Kwame Nkrumah, the famed pan-Africanist and first prime minister and president of Ghana, also graduated from Lincoln University and went on to incite powerful change in his home country.

These figures in our far and recent history represent the sector of service that is activism. Activism is service that transcends the bounds of the status quo or the maintenance of already existing structures. Instead, activists are workers in service of change, and they bring forth new ideas and movements that they believe will affect the greatest good for their communities.

Without Black activists in this country, many of the freedoms that we all enjoy would not be so readily accessible. Without Black colleges, many of the activists who work so hard to ensure these freedoms for all would not have had the spaces and opportunities to grow their character and develop their beliefs. They also would not have had the platforms and organizational networks necessary to enact change and proliferate new ideas throughout the world.

The names I lift up in this chapter are names of people whose influence and impact extend well beyond the walls of our schools. I introduce this history to illustrate the fact that HBCUs, their faculty and student bodies, have always answered the call to service and to activism. Furthermore, through them, the spirits of our institutions have been carried like seeds across the globe and gone on to reproduce movements for freedom, equality, justice, and a better world.

CHAPTER 5

MORAL COMPASS

Many folks of my generation have a great concern for the state of morality today, and I think there's been lots of miscommunication as to why. Morality is not purely about control for control's sake or exerting power over others. At their best, systems of morality are ways that we can govern ourselves and have sovereignty individually and collectively.

Your moral compass is what you use to determine your choices and the way you will live. It is the way that you decide what is right, wrong, or in-between, and this system is how you determine your own answers to moral questions. Not everyone's moral system is the same, nor should everyone's moral systems be based on the same things. I believe in diversity of thought and values. I use my Christian faith as a base for my moral code, but what you select to guide you can be up to you. The point is that you find for yourself a better way to live.

Moral codes are important, because without them we risk betraying our own values. We also risk making decisions that harm others, or that lack consideration for greater issues outside our immediate feelings or opinions. Your moral code is what pushes you to speak up when you witness an injustice. It is also what moves you to apologize when you've made a mistake or transgressed another person's boundaries. Our moral code is what helps us to choose the best course of action, and it's important that along with strong character and work ethic, we develop moral codes that bring us closer to the kind of people we want to be and the kind of world we want to live in.

Moral Tools to Guide You

Personally, I like to simplify things, and I find that the Ten Commandments always help me to find my way. If I'm not living according to this code, more than likely things are going awry in my life. We may sometimes think that following rules makes us feel like we are being controlled, or that we don't have the ability and free will to do what we want. However, I think there are always opportunities to use the Ten Commandments and apply them to our lives in new ways. Here's my interpretation of how the Ten Commandments can be used to provide moral guidance today.

1. Thou shall have no other gods before me nor worship false idols.	1. Maintain Your Priorities and Deal in What's Real.
2. Thou shall not take the Lord's name in vain.	2. Be Serious with Your Words.
3. Remember to keep the Sabbath day holy.	3. Make Time for What Is Sacred and Holy.
4. Honor thy father and mother.	4. Honor Those Who Came Before You.
5. Thou shall not kill.	5. Bring Life to All You Do.

6. Thou shall not commit adultery.	6. Respect the Boundaries of Others.
7. Thou shall not steal.	7. Have Integrity in Your Work.
8. Thou shall not lie.	8. Commit to a Relationship with the Truth.
9. Thou shall not covet your neighbor's wife.	9. Focus on Yourself and Cherish What You've Got.
10. Thou shall not covet your neighbor's goods.	10. Take Care of Your Own Business.

Maintain Your Priorities

Maintaining your priorities means developing a sense of what is most and least important. It's not always easy. We don't always know how to classify what's most important all the time, and different seasons of our lives may require more or less commitment in different areas of our lives. Yet, there are some things that should always hold the most prized place in our lives. For me, it's my relationship with God and my family. They come first in my life! Whatever your God, whoever your God, maintain your steadfast commitment to this entity, and hold fast to your priorities, which will guide your actions.

Deal in What's Real

False idols are all over the place today, even though we wouldn't name them as such. Folks worship money, status, and illusions. I believe part of not worshipping false idols is about being able to determine what is real and what's not, and making sure that we prioritize what is real above all else. Are the priorities you've picked for yourself leading you to where you actually want to go? Are the things you treat with the greatest importance of benefit to your best life or are they undermining your advancement? Weed out what's not real, so that you can focus on what is.

Be Serious with Your Words

Taking the Lord's name in vain is about being serious when you speak. No matter your spiritual beliefs, your words are important, and they are powerful. Speaking with wisdom and being serious about what you say is an important aspect of building a strong moral character. Your integrity and reputation are built, in many ways, by the words that you say. Be mindful of the words that you use, what you say, and how you say it.

Make Time for What Is Sacred and Holy

Keeping the holy day may mean something different to every reader, but I believe that time spent to take care of one's spiritual and mental state is important. It's critical to connect with what is sacred and holy, however we define those things. Time management is part of having a good work ethic, and also a part of having a holistic and balanced life. Make choices that help you to manage your time and take care of what is most important. When you use this to guide your decision-making, you are putting your well-being first, and this will always serve you well.

Honor Those Who Came Before You

Honor those who came before you—this may be your parents, your ancestors, or the people whose legacy you walk in, ideologically. The people who came before you in your field of study or work have also left inheritances for you, and it's important to remember this so that you can honor their contributions and continue in the work that is left to be done. When caught in difficult moral decisions, it can help to think about those you admire, respect, and believe in. Think about the values that you share with these people and choose what is most aligned with the wisdom and guidance that has already been cultivated for you.

Bring Life to All You Do

It's pretty clear that killing isn't a great moral choice. I think sometimes what we don't question on the other side of this commandment is a will to bring life into all that we do. Bringing life means speaking positively and optimistically. It means bringing a bright and ready attitude and a will to grow in all circumstances. Don't tread on others, and don't work destructively against the work of others. Bring life by bringing your best. When you live by this moral standard, your life is bound to be fruitful.

Respect the Boundaries of Others

Learning and navigating boundaries is one of the most challenging and fulfilling lessons of life. When we understand our own boundaries and the boundaries of others, we learn how we want to be treated, and how others ought to be treated as well. The commandment that speaks to not committing adultery is an excellent example of crossing a boundary. However, there are numerous other boundaries and commitments that we should not cross, no matter how tempting it may be. A moral respect for boundaries helps us to make choices that protect our

commitments to ourselves and others and reinforces the values
that we hold. Respect others, and respect yourself.

Have Integrity in Your Work

When you've worked hard for something, you don't like others
picking at it, sampling from it, or duplicating it. Why would this
be different for anyone else? Have integrity in your work and
maintain a moral reputation for being authentic in what you do.
Taking from others robs you of the chance to create something
for yourself, and to gain what you need from your own experiences. Don't rob yourself of that chance by robbing someone else.

Commit to a Relationship with the Truth

As I discussed in the earlier chapter on character, I believe it's
important to develop a strong commitment and relationship
with the truth. The truth is not always easy to parse out, but
when we search for righteousness, we can find solutions that
bring us closer to justice and honesty. As you live your life, walking with the truth will serve you well. It will reinforce your good
name and reputation in all that you undertake.

Focus on Yourself and Cherish What You've Got

When we covet others' belongings, we're not giving ourselves
the chance to cherish what we have ourselves. I think the un-
spoken aspect of this commandment to resist envy is to also embrace gratitude. Minding our own business and being deeply
thankful for the things we have can be the best antidote to feelings of jealousy or envy. When you feel tempted to look too hard
at what others have going on, recenter yourself on the blessings

and good things going on in your life. It will help you gain a more optimistic perspective, or at the very least remind you of things you can feel good about for yourself.

Mind Your Own Business

The commandment that speaks to not coveting your neighbors' goods means that we should mind our own business. Minding your own business is a full-time job that requires you to commit your time and attention to taking care of the things that impact your life personally and professionally. If you work consistently to complete tasks that lead to the accomplishment of your goals, you will not have time to concern yourself with how others live their lives and conduct their business. Staying out of other people's business allows you more time to attend to your own.

Let Your Values Lead the Way

Determining right from wrong is a contentious endeavor. The state of legal and political systems around the world will always attest to that. What has become increasingly challenging to watch is how general sentiments today have taken a drastic and persistent shift toward nihilism.

Nihilism is a philosophical viewpoint that denies the existence of objective truth, and especially of moral truths. I am concerned that our society, and especially our youngest members of society, are entrenched in a battle with nihilism, and the belief that because nothing matters, and all systems are corrupt, then anything is permissible and personal responsibility for actions is unnecessary or unreasonable. On the other side of this attitude, we also have a generation of people who are hypersensitive and militant about the issues that matter most to them, but rigid, callous, and unyielding when engaging with the views of others. The media we consume only polarizes these attitudes and, as a result, the flow of moral ideas and the development of moral values have been disturbed.

Dr. Cornel West once wrote that "nihilism is a national consequence of a culture (or civilization) ruled and regulated by categories that mask manipulation, mastery, and domination of people and nature." If that's not what's going on today, then I don't know what is. I do believe in hope for our future and maintain that with every choice a person has before them, there is an opportunity for their moral beliefs to be built up.

The hope that I hold for the future comes directly from the past. What we come to know for sure when we study the past is that people change, and so do civilizations. Even empires are fluctuating structures that rise and fall. Ideas flow from place to place, and power changes hands according to the themes and lessons of the times. Some lessons come around and revolutionize the world and remain with us through centuries, while others rise and fall like the seasons and wither away. Not to get too poetic about it, but what we can see when we look at history is that society changes. I draw my hope for a better world from history, which shows me that change is a constant fact of our world. The fatalistic and nihilistic attitude espoused by many today is not rooted in history, though it pretends to be. It is true that humans will likely always be engaged in struggles for power and fairness, but our attitudes in the face of this struggle ought to be anchored in optimism; our investments ought to be in love and hope for a better future.

This is another reason why HBCUs and their place in the world are so powerful to me. As a graduate and leader of historically Black institutions, I know that what Black people have to offer one another and the world is worth more than gold. We have so much to give and so much potential to reach. I also know that for many who walk our halls and campuses, the first time they are granted a more encompassing view of our great history and legacy in this country is when they matriculate into school around the age of eighteen years old. This is the first time they get to learn about themselves and be the center of their learning experiences. It is the first time that they experience Black professors and scholars with doctoral degrees and deep knowledge of our contributions to the world. There is so much that many young people growing up today don't know about themselves because the greater K–12 national education system does not teach it. I am grateful to HBCUs and their place as strongholds in education, training, and culture. Yet, I know that the first time a young boy or girl learns about Ida B. Wells or Arturo Schomburg, Bayard Rustin or Ella Baker, doesn't have to be at university. The first time we learn about ourselves in depth doesn't have to be on an HBCU campus either. We can create and reproduce safe havens of learning and uplift Black people of any age and social status. It can be done. It requires that we are intentional about transferring what we know to be true and cultivating the opportunities to do so.

I recently learned of one young woman who took on a powerful project in the school where she worked. This HBCU alumna, whom we will call Chanel, stumbled into her role as an English language arts educator in a Harlem charter school in New York City. When she began working at this school, housed in the historic birthplace of the Harlem Renaissance, she noticed that many of her students detested reading. Upon further inspection, Chanel also observed a woeful lack of diverse literature on her classroom and library bookshelves.

"Why does our bookshelf look like this?" Chanel asked herself. "We're in Harlem!"

She became very vocal about representation with her supervisors and principal. The school listened and expanded the budget to rebuild and develop the library with more diverse books for students and teachers to use.

Chanel continued to think about what her students needed to be truly prepared and successful in the world they would one day be leading. She remembered her own K–12 experience and noted that while she had other supportive Black communities in her life to draw from, she lacked the kind of instruction at school that would have affirmed her in her traditional education. She also remembered the first time at her alma mater that her professor passed out a syllabus including only works written by African American and African diaspora authors. She was shocked! If she were at a predominantly white institution, it would not have surprised her to review a syllabus with exclusively white authors. Somehow, a list of Black authors was a novelty. This reality is unfair, and it exists in an overwhelming majority of our nation's educational institutions. Furthermore, this injustice does not only affect the students who feel invisible due to exclusionary curriculum. It also negatively impacts and influences all students who are educated in a system that fails to reflect the fullness and diversity of American work and history.

For Chanel, going to an HBCU was the first time in her educational career that she was able to embrace her race and embrace her history, to learn about herself and for that to be okay. She did not want this to be the case for her students, especially when they walked daily down the same streets that many of our most influential culture makers, activists, and writers once walked.

"I want to give the students that *now* and especially because they're in Harlem," Chanel said.

"Harlem is another mecca, but [my students] unfortunately don't know the history behind their neighborhood and how critical it was to the Black community and the Black experience. They are inundated with what they see on the news and what they see around them that doesn't necessarily point to that legacy."

She spoke with her supervisors and devised a plan for how to introduce more diverse subjects into the curriculum. While working at the school, she was also studying to earn her master's degree in education. As a teaching fellow, she was given the opportunity to create and teach an African American literature course, and as part of that course, a project called "HBCU week." Chanel came into education as an English major, not as an educational professional, so she didn't exactly understand the realities or anticipate some of the obstacles she would face in the field of education. She experienced microaggressions and ignorance from her colleagues—both Black and white—who didn't fully understand the value of her projects.

Before the implementation of the African American literature course and HBCU week, one of her colleagues commented
that she felt HBCUs "didn't reflect real life." Another recounted
hearsay from others who felt HBCUs were "too Black." These
attitudes only steeled Chanel's resolve. She felt a moral obliga-
tion to follow through with her plans and to make sure that her
students had as many opportunities to learn about themselves
as possible. Despite the isolation she felt, she decided that the
most important thing to focus on was doing the right thing for
the students in her classroom.

"Coming from an HBCU, I don't feel the need to prove myself to people, or prove the validity of the institution, but for the
sake of the children, we did that. I loved being able to show both
them and the adults watching just how critical HBCUs were
and still are."

In addition to developing a reading curriculum based on
African American writers and works, Chanel tapped into her
HBCU network to develop a video series on HBCUs that could
be shown to students of all ages in her school. During HBCU
week, twenty different alumni from different schools explained
the history of their universities and their personal experiences.
They also discussed how the schools were important parts of
American history, and how they played a role in many of the
freedoms that we all enjoy today. A lot of this information was
new to the staff and teachers, too.

"Especially when it came to *Brown versus Board of Education*,
the landmark case that desegregated schools, that was the most
exciting time to point to," Chanel said. "That fight did not only
benefit African Americans. It benefitted anybody of color, and

that fight emerged out of the HBCUs. I could point to figures in history like Martin Luther King Jr., the most recognizable civil rights icon, and say 'This is a product of an HBCU.' I think that the initiative was successful in waking some people up to the legacy behind education in the Black community."

Against pressures to conform, and to be pessimistic about what the future holds, a sense of morality can guide our steps toward a better way to live. I believe this is the true power of a moral code and compass. As people who have been endowed with talent and given the tools to build a better and more equitable world, a moral code enables us to act responsibly and honorably. It also provides a clear conscience even as we wade through the gray area of life's cloudy situations.

For Chanel, this is ultimately what allowed her to push through the challenge of HBCU week, and to do what she knew was right for her students. "I decided to focus on what I could control and my direct influence, which is my classroom," she said. "I could leave education today and be satisfied because I feel like I always honored my moral code of the project that I did."

CHAPTER 6

HIGH GOALS, BIG DREAMS

I always tell the people I encounter to have high goals and to dream no small dreams. As is often said, there are no limits to what you can accomplish except the limits you place on yourself. Belief in your own abilities and a strong desire to achieve is an important pillar of success. So I encourage all young people to cultivate a strong sense of ambition and watch as life takes on new meaning and purpose. Think to yourself about the last time you had a dream or a goal that ignited your drive and propelled you forward. Is that flame still burning in your life?

Cultivate YOUR Ambition

Each person's motivation for moving toward goals is different. The things that will sustain my drive and career may not be enough to sustain someone else. As with most things we've been discussing in this book, there is an element of personal reflection that is necessary for dreaming big dreams and achieving great goals.

Lots of people have borrowed ambition. They look around them, consider the popular choices, and select the goals and motivations that "everyone" is meant to aspire to. Instead of doing the hard work of inner reflection and being visionaries for their own life, many people simply follow the scripts that have been prepared for them to act out. It's sometimes simpler and easier to look everywhere but inside ourselves for guidance. That is, until you find yourself in impassable conflict with who you really are! Borrowed ambition can lead you down pathways you should never have stepped foot upon. It can have you underplaying your skills and holding yourself back to fit into an ideal that's not a true match for your talent, or it can have you completely stressed out and trying to keep up with the Joneses. Your goals and dreams must be your own so that they can properly sustain you through the trials of success and achievement.

Because of this delicate balance between motivation and success, I consider a healthy sense of ambition to be linked to a person's character and integrity. Whatever your goals, ambition calls for you to be true to your capacity and potential. Ambition pushes you to not settle for less, to always think bigger, and to test the limits of what you think you can do and who you think you can be. Ambitious people are intent on not letting their talent and opportunities spoil before they have a chance to exploit all their personal potential. When a person's motivations are in the right place, meaning in alignment with their true goals and purpose, that person is much more able to hurdle the challenges that may arise. Borrowed ambition or misplaced ambition will not be enough when you are facing failures and hard lessons, dealing with disappointment, or struggling to find a way out of a problem when there's no clear path to take. A strong sense of integrity can help you in these moments, to find your way back to the truth and to forge through difficulty to find success.

Think deeply about what motivates you, and what kind of life and work you are toiling toward. When you are being honest about this, you can also dig deeper into your talents and detect areas of interest and passion that you might not have been aware of. At HBCUs, young students learn about ambition through their exposure to others working big jobs, with big dreams and goals. Students at HBCUs are striving to build businesses, write books, and mount projects together. The environment is such that these ideas aren't considered too outlandish! At an HBCU, you are surrounded by people who believe in Black people's capacity to be great at everything and anything. It is a place where you can be anything, do anything, and go anywhere you want to go, and still be Black. Black folks dreaming and doing things that are not "traditional" are still going for their goals with all their might. There are painters, artists, athletes, economists, and politicians, exposing themselves to the kinds of dreams that they can have, and expanding those dreams according to their great talent and ambition. Sometimes, university students can even take on more than they can chew, and they exhaust themselves academically and socially trying to pursue all the things on their schedules. The beauty is that they can be exposed to different ideas, experiences, and knowledge that will be invaluable to the lives they choose later on. Self-awareness and self-confidence that build and reinforce ambition are fostered very well at our schools.

Not Always What, but How

Sometimes the limits we place on ourselves seem well thought-out and practical. You might say, "I want to be a doctor." This may be a useful and definitive goal that helps you to plan out your life. Yet, when we focus too much on WHAT we want to be instead of HOW we want to live, complications can arise. Perhaps you say you would like to be a doctor but you haven't yet thought more critically about what a doctor must do in his or her day-to-day life. Do you want to be regularly on-call? Do you want to deal with insurance claims? Do you know what a doctor's life is really like, and if you do, would you still choose this career? This is not at all to dissuade the reader from aspiring to certain goals, especially those generally deemed lucrative, honorable, or worthy of pursuit. Rather, I think many professionals at certain moments in their careers can become rigid in their idea of what success and ambition in their lives ought to look like, because they haven't really interrogated their motivations to see what really matters to them in life.

Beyond the soul searching that often happens in higher education, the evolution of our dreams and goals continues. Many professionals in the world today studied in preparation for careers that, once they landed jobs in their intended fields, were not the right fit for them. While this can be a discouraging realization, it is also the chance to dream bigger and invite new goals, passions, and dreams to grow in our lives. The world is constantly changing when it comes to work and work-life balance, and we must change with it. As a result of the coronavirus pandemic, a large part of what our global industries had to learn, and are continuing to struggle with, is how to adapt and find the best fit in a constantly changing set of circumstances. As you set down your path toward the life and career you desire, remember that this journey is about trying things out to find what works, and it's not ever going to be an exact science. With each new experience, we gain more information about who we are and what kind of life we want to have.

If You're Being Bad, Be the Baddest

Once you've examined your motivations, determined your goals, and set forth toward your dreams, you must now put all your energy toward reaching the achievements and the life you want to have.

"If you're being bad, be the baddest," Katherine Johnson laughingly said at Hampton's commencement ceremony in 2017. I laughed, too, hearing these words and understanding the truth in them. To me, Mrs. Johnson meant you should strive to be the very best that you can be. Commitment to your goals and ambitions is not always easy, but when you have decided who you want to be and what you want to do, go forward with full force. Be the best. Be the best that you can be! Your dreams are yours, and so are your motivations. Remain true to the passions and talent you have by honoring them with your fullest effort.

CHAPTER 7

BE COLLABORATIVE AND COMPETITIVE

HBCUs Are Competitive Institutions

More often than I care to admit, I hear from both Black and white folk alike that HBCUs don't adequately prepare their students for the "real world." The truth is that HBCUs were born of the very serious reality that our nation still struggles to accept and integrate Black people into society with true equity and equality. Considering that reality, HBCUs offer a competitive education for students of all backgrounds deserving of training and opportunity. While I can go on forever about how our professors and course offerings are comparable in every way to what you may find at any other predominantly white institution, I must reiterate that the greatest lesson any student of an HBCU learns is that they are worthy of support, mentorship, and community. They also learn how to be in and create support, mentorship, and community for themselves, and how to integrate these relationships into their lives once they have graduated from a university setting. This kind of community building, networking, and, ultimately, collaboration that occurs on our campuses is what I believe truly makes our students competitive.

Collaborative Attitude, Competitive Edge

Collaboration is a competitive skill. You may not think it to be so at first, but one of the most important factors in a person's success on the job is an ability to work well with others. Whether you work for an employer or work for yourself, whether you work on a team or have a team of your own beneath you, all work is collaborative in nature. No person is successful entirely on his own. This is another lesson that many HBCU students learn through various experiences on campus, and I believe these lessons translate very easily to the working world as well.

You might have seen a good Spike Lee movie or watched all seasons of *A Different World* and now imagine that you know what goes down on the yard at an HBCU. In reality, what's going on when students and professors come together from so many diverse backgrounds and fields of study is often a combination of a natural melting together and intentional efforts to develop community and harmony. The social organizations on campus, and the rites of passage that they offer students, are part of forming the sort of collaborative spirit that will ultimately serve students in their professional endeavors going forward. Even some residential halls at various HBCUs have social organizations whose aims are to teach their members not only important professional and personal development skills, but also a sense of fraternity that is necessary for working well with others. Why does a residence hall need a step team? Why do marching bands need fraternities? Why do Black people need Greek letter organizations? One of many answers is that our ability to relate to, connect with, and collaborate with one another is facilitated by these sorts of endeavors. We all need to learn how to be collaborative in one way or another, and this does not come naturally all the time.

Consider a student who has joined the marching band at an HBCU. HBCUs have some of the most iconic and influential marching band cultures in the world, and our student musicians are some of the most talented in the nation. When it comes time to prepare for big performances, be it homecoming games or presidential inaugurations, these students must work together to develop a performance worthy of their university's name. What we see on the field during half-time shows is the result of weeks of preparation. Music has been written, choreography has been mapped out, and musicians must cooperate to find the rhythm, and to put on a show that will move the athletes and spectators with joy and good music. As a part of the crowd, you may simply think of these marching bands as entertainment between segments of the game. What these types of social interactions offer students behind the scenes is the chance to lead, to make plans together, to manage conflict, and to learn how to prioritize a good collective outcome over individual differences. No matter where you go next in life, these skills will translate well and be beneficial to both employee and employer.

In the classroom as well, students of many disciplines get the chance to collaborate with one another and develop the sorts of soft skills necessary for success in any given field or career. Hampton's business school is known for producing great collaborative leaders in business, who can work together to bring projects to life. They are trained to be this way! Our students are often grouped into teams during their first year of study, where they work together and learn together. This experience is an essential part of learning how to be part of a team, and to bring out the best in your teammates so that the final product can really shine. An emphasis on collaboration is important in business, but also in most areas and industries where people must come together to do work and make projects reality.

What our students learn in our classrooms is that their collaborative skills are actually their competitive edge. When they graduate and move on to work in companies and on teams with other people from other schools, they are trained in working cooperatively. They bring their best to the teams they are on and put forth a collaborative spirit that brings life to each project they are a part of. When you think about it, everyone wants a collaborative person on their team. You want someone who is going to be positive about doing great work, and someone who is going to listen attentively and participate actively. You want people on your team who will raise concerns as well as solutions and do their best to make sure that the team looks good, not just themselves. There are moments and situations where it's important to be self-interested, and to make sure that your own needs are being met. However, I have come to understand that collaboration is profoundly linked to success in any lasting endeavor, and employers and entrepreneurs are always seeking this kind of powerfully positive energy in their organizations.

The world teaches us to be self-interested, to look out for ourselves and develop a competitive edge that eclipses community and maximizes personal achievement. Yet, when we consider history and the legacy of visionaries and change-makers, it is in collective efforts to transform the world that successes have been won. I don't think that this is a fluke or coincidence. When we come together and lift as we climb, we practice collaborative attitudes with one another and develop a stronger community for ourselves and for future generations.

Mentorship

Mentorship is such an essential part of growth in any area of life. Without mentorship, we are lost up a creek without a paddle. Truly this is what I believe. Mentorship is a kind of collaboration that we overlook sometimes. We create a section called "acknowledgments" for our life and pull it out when it's time to make a speech about the help we have received along the way to our successes. Do we talk enough about how to cultivate mentorship relationships, and the importance of this in our everyday culture and community building? I know that I would not be where I am today if it were not for the mentorship and guidance I received from my parents, family, faith community, and academic communities. I also see after years of leading in university settings how schools are amazing places because of their unique offering of mentorship and guidance for students and future leaders.

Mentorship is influence, guidance, and direction from one person to another. It can also be encouragement, correction, and collaboration. Mentorship is a sort of behind-the-scenes collaboration that happens in the development of an individual. When you welcome mentorship into your life, you allow the influence of another person to shape who you are. A mentor can help you to create opportunities for yourself and help you navigate situations you might not be equipped to handle on your own. Your mentor works with you to bring out the best in you, and this is a kind of collaboration that requires investment from both sides. Someone pouring advice and help into your life is only beneficial if you are open to receive what is being offered. Mentorship is collaboration, and I believe it makes the difference for any person at any stage of their career.

It is most definitely up to you to have ambition and to be able to drive your own career forward. No one else is going to be more serious about getting you the opportunities and experience that you need to make things work out for you. In many ways, the folks around you can only help you as much as you are willing to help yourself, and as much as you know yourself. It's your life! Yet, there are also people out there in your community and network looking to help when and where they can. Others can provide the best help and support when they know where you want to go and what goals you have for your life and career. If we are clear about our goals and intentions, we can ask for what we need and receive help through relationships, networks, and mentorship.

Some folks may be hesitant to ask for help for a number of reasons. Skipping the line or getting in the door through personal connections can be uncomfortable for some, and nepotism in this world has often worked against Black people. So it makes sense that we can feel conflict about accepting help in a rigged system where we are told that we must always succeed on our own merits and earn our place like everyone else. We know that merit is not the sole factor at play when it comes to career ascension—not for our counterparts and not for us either! Black folks need to leverage their networks just like everyone else. We need to make sure that mentorship and lifting others up as we climb remain standard professional practice in our culture.

Part of taking all the opportunities to shine means building relationships that will help you to shine. Seek relationships with folks who know your work, believe in your capacity, and are willing to give you a chance, or sometimes many chances. A relationship with a professor or university faculty member can be a lifelong lifeline. These mentors can provide letters of recommendation and simple guidance toward opportunities in your given field or related fields of study. This is also true for former employers, and people you may encounter who you admire and connect with at different moments in your career. We often don't keep in regular touch in ways that could make a difference, and then sometimes we feel at a loss for help when we find ourselves in need. The great thing is that it is never too late to reach out to someone you trust, as long as you're both standing on God's green earth. There are so many ways that you can build your community and leverage networks that you already have. You may be well past the moment of reaching out to former teachers, but what about the potential mentors and guiding stars present in the company your work for, or the networks that you are a part of? Are you actively seeking out career-boosting opportunities like fellowships, conferences, and training? As you seek growth, you will encounter others who are also seeking growth for themselves and who may be farther along the road than you are. You will also encounter elders who are chock-full of wisdom and insight, and ready to share what they've learned with the next generation.

Another collaborative aspect of mentorship is legacy, though we don't always consider it this way. When you open yourself up to mentorship, you participate in the transfer of knowledge that places you in a lineage. The knowledge you apply to yourself comes from somewhere, and with each generation that knowledge is passed down and preserved. It is a beautiful privilege to have access to guidance. For this reason, I believe we ought to seek it when we need it and share it generously with others, too. Just as you have been endowed with information, consider how you can engage in a spirit of collaboration by reaching out to others who may need support, and making yourself available for those coming after you. Learning is not just a top-down experience, and we can often learn a lot about our own perspectives when we look to engage with those who are younger than us. Find ways to share as much as you receive and seek out opportunities to grow your network wide and large. We need one another to succeed, and we are much stronger both individually and collectively when we remember this.

Put yourself in the places where advancement is happening and be intentional about building relationships wherever you go. Remain open about what you want for yourself and seek out the help and support that you need to achieve the goals and life you desire. You are a much more competitive individual when you carry a spirit of partnership and when you welcome collaborative community in your professional life.

CHAPTER 8

DEALING WITH DISTRACTIONS

Distractions are sneaky and unavoidable things. I say *unavoidable* because ignoring the things that are stealing away our focus is not always all it takes to overcome them. In many instances, and, I would argue, in the most important instances, managing distractions is about being able to face up to them, say "no" to them, and reframe our attention back to the things we are intent on working toward.

A distraction to me is anything that diverts your attention and focus from a task at hand or negatively alters an established plan or goal. It can also be something that causes interruptions and disturbances in your mental state. Distractions are not always malignant, but given too much room to roam free, distractions can eat away at your focus and be a great hindrance to reaching your goals. After so many words about character, vision, ambition, and preparation, it's important to consider the things that get in the way of all our plans and cause us to lose sight of our purpose and future.

Having served as president of a university for over forty years, I have seen time and time again how critical of a skill it is to be able to navigate distractions well. Newly minted young adults walking onto an HBCU campus are a little bit like children walking into a candy shop with a few bucks in hand. There are so many things to do, and only four years to sample every experience. When the consequences of distractions begin to rear their ugly heads, students soon learn that the "try it all" approach is not a good enough plan for success. After sampling activities to determine what we enjoy and what is best for us, we must develop plans and strategies for making our goals happen.

Distractions are an incessant reality, especially in today's age. There are so many things vying for our attention and energy at any given moment, and so many things our society holds us accountable for knowing. Navigating these pressures and intrusions on our attention is difficult, but I believe we can all manage to maintain control of our attention and protect our goals through discipline, wisdom, and healthy priorities.

Discipline

We need discipline to ensure that work gets done. Without it, we will quickly fall off from our routines and compromise our goals when the work gets hard, or when we get tired. Working for the life you want will demand sacrifice! There will always be temptation to quit and give up or to be lazy and less diligent. When you know you've got a great vision for your life and have already worked out the plan to bring you closer to achievement, a disciplined lifestyle will support you and enable you to follow through with your goals.

Though challenging to embody, discipline is the ability to choose the best thing for you. It requires being able to choose and consistently act in your own interest. When you are faced with temptation to make a lesser choice over a better one, what you want to focus on is how the better choice benefits you, why it is good for you, and how this choice fits into your long-term goals. Our goals can be derailed by distractions, but if we can build a routine that reinforces them, we will make consistent decisions that promote the achievement of our plans. Having discipline in your life does not mean that distractions won't arise, or that you won't struggle to make the best choices. It does, however, provide a strong foundation for your ability to do so. Discipline represents an investment in the work that you are doing and shows your seriousness concerning that invest-ment. If you can prove to yourself that you are willing to make the choices that benefit you, you are more likely to prevail over distractions that come your way.

Discipline is also helpful in learning and correcting poor choices and habits by adopting better ones. When we lack matu-rity, it's tempting to think of discipline as an external thing that happens to us, like a punishment or a negative force against our own desires. When we embrace discipline as a value that brings us closer to our goals, it also leads us to correction, and helps us to find better ways to navigate problems like distractions. When you turn challenges like distractions into learning opportuni-ties, you make way for wisdom to enter your life.

Wisdom

Proverbs 19:20 says, "listen to advice and accept discipline, and at the end you will be counted among the wise." I agree wholeheartedly that through discipline and advice, wisdom is developed.

Wisdom is the ability to discern or judge what is true or right. Wisdom provides a person with a good sense of judgement, and offers insight that helps to inform one's outlook, attitudes, and decisions. Wisdom is gained through experience, and it can be passed on through communication, storytelling, and sharing knowledge. Wisdom is often hard won but it doesn't have to be. As a parent, mentor, and leader, I am always seeking to impart what I've learned through my own fumbles and journeys to those who could make use of that information. This is why engaging in mentorship relationships is important, and why learning in communities with people of different backgrounds, ages, and worldviews can make a person more well-rounded and equipped to navigate life. You don't have to reinvent the wheel, and you don't have to repair the wheel on your own. Wisdom that has been cultivated by others is also there for you to utilize, so find those sources of knowledge and guidance to help you.

Being able to discern wisely also reinforces our ability to navigate distractions, because we are better able to identify choices as good for us or bad for us. Even for the most disciplined, hardworking, and visionary people, it can be hard to figure out the best course of action when dealing with distractions. Not all distractions are easily identified as such. In fact, just like anything else, what we consider a distraction is a deeply personal determination. We can all be drawn to things that are seemingly good but ultimately compromising for our long-term goals for achievement.

Consider a university student who has joined a sport team. Athletics are great and offer opportunities for so many pertinent lessons about life and success. Athletes learn about discipline and time management. They learn how to take care of their bodies and stay active. Playing on a team can also provide great social skills and soft skills that can be useful in networking and collaboration with others. Sports can be an amazing chance for a person to grow and develop. For the wrong person at the wrong time, they can also be a major distraction.

Imagine that you play sports and you're up for a career-enhancing fellowship that requires a certain grade point average. You might need to employ wisdom to discern the best choices for your goals. In the face of a tough decision, perhaps you will ask for advice from a mentor or friend on what to do. Perhaps they will pray, or do research on their own to see what others have done in the same situation. Ultimately, you will discover that while sports are not inherently distracting, continuing to engage in sports at this time might pose a problem for your greater life goals. Anything can be a distraction when it is getting in the way of your primary aims. For this reason, we must employ wisdom and sort out our priorities. For when we do so, we can determine what truly matters and face distractions once and for all.

In my lifetime, I have had mentors who have literally enhanced my being. These individuals include Mr. K. B. Young, my high school principal and friend; Dr. Edgar Toppin, my major professor at Virginia State University and the first African American I knew who had written a book; Dr. Ted Sizer, my major professor and dean at Harvard; and Dr. Luther Foster, who was president of Tuskegee University when I was administrative vice president. All of these mentors contributed to my personal and professional growth in a manner for which I will be eternally grateful.

Priorities

I believe that healthy priorities are values that help us rank the merit of different activities or endeavors. The fact of the matter is that we only have so many hours accorded to our lives, and our time is our most valuable resource. When we develop priorities, we become aware of this reality, and of all the seemingly important things competing for our prized and precious time. Our priorities can be healthy or unhealthy depending on how well they help us do our work and complete our objectives. For example, prioritizing friendships with others is extremely important. Friendships are a part of what makes life meaningful, and strong community is important for fulfillment and success. However, one must be able to rank the importance of friendship against the other things and interests that may be competing for energy and attention in one's life. I may have arranged with a friend to be out and to do a planned activity together. I appreciate my friend and enjoy spending time with him. I don't want to miss out on what this social interaction has to offer, and I also may just be needing some time to have fun and be in the company of others. At the same time, if conflict arises in my priorities, I must be able to choose wisely. I might have an important deadline to meet and be unsure of my ability to both enjoy myself socially and complete my work. I must be able to understand my situation and make a decision that serves me. The choice I make will be an indication of my priorities, and the choices I make will consistently determine the lifestyle I lead overall.

Priorities are important for this reason. They allow us to determine objectively and according to our own values what is most important to us. Unhealthy priorities will place greater importance on the things that undermine our well-being, and they will lead us to giving in to our distractions. Meanwhile, healthy priorities protect the work and investment that we have made in ourselves. They will also reflect the powerful and positive impact of discipline and wisdom in our lives.

CHAPTER 9

MAKING IT HAPPEN, START TO FINISH

Start Where You Are

Starting where you are is the best and honestly the only place to begin. We all have a long list of things we'd like to fix before we'll be finally *ready* to do something big in our lives. We say, *when I'm wealthier, when I'm more stable, when I'm less busy.* We put qualifiers on our starting blocks and then wonder why we never finish the race. To get off the starting block, you've got to be willing to give yourself a chance, and you've got to decide that you are worthy of it.

When I think about what it means to make a new start right where you are, I think about Booker T. Washington's famous controversial speech at the Atlanta Exposition on September 18th, 1895. That speech was the first of its kind in many ways, and it goes down in history as being a divisive point of contention for Black political leaders even to this day. Booker T. Washington was a man who believed wholeheartedly in evolution through education. He studied at Hampton University, and he was a devoted and determined student—he arrived at the university on foot. When he left Hampton, he went on to establish the Tuskegee Institute, now Tuskegee University, in Alabama, a technical school founded firstly on trade and mechanical education.

In his speech, Washington recounted the story of a vessel stranded at sea and desperate for aid. The ship sighted another vessel in the distance and sent out a distress call saying, "Water, water. We die of thirst." The signal from the friendly vessel returned a message: *Cast down your buckets where you are.* The distressed ship, unwilling to believe that the waters below them would be suitable to drink, continued to repeat the same message, and to receive the same answer. *Cast down your buckets where you are.* Finally, the vessel cast down its buckets, and it found them filled with fresh water from the Amazon River.

More common interpretations of this allegory carry the weight of our country's racial history and don't always reflect the essence of what I believe Washington hoped to convey to those who heard him. Some have taken this speech to mean a diminishing of African Americans' capacities to engage in work beyond the technical and mechanical labor of the working class. Others see it as a speech that overly burdens Black folks without holding whites accountable to the task of equitable reconstruction. When I consider the contributions that came from Tuskegee Institute, and the critical importance of mechanical and manual labor in the world we live in, I believe that Washington had more than appeasing white sensibilities on his mind when he spoke on that September day.

Dying of thirst in the middle of a freshwater river sounds like a mighty sad fate when you think about it. Sometimes we deprive ourselves of new beginnings and of fresh starts because we don't believe that our current situation can afford us the freedom we want. We haven't always taken stock of what's around us to truly explore our options. I won't say that it's simple work, or that there is always a ready solution to tap into. Sometimes we believe that the only salvation available to us somehow lies in the hands of someone else, somewhere else. We don't feel empowered in our situations, and we think that if we could just be in someone else's shoes or get the resources that someone else has, we would be better capable of fixing whatever problems we have at hand. If we are not results-oriented in difficult situations, what makes us think we will fare better when given more resources? Problems are always going to arise. In the constant tumult of life, we may at times discover ourselves stuck between rocks and hard places, unable to find the best way out, around, or through. If we first consider ourselves empowered instead of disempowered, we can begin to think more resourcefully, and craft solutions that bring us closer to a fresh start. I think the message to *cast your bucket where you may* is a fine piece of advice for someone feeling unable to see the opportunities right in front of their faces.

Plan for the Life You Want

Starting from where you are is one thing, and it's a very significant first decision to make. Moving forward, it's also important to plan for the life that you want. While you shouldn't stop living because you're waiting for everything to be perfect, you should always devise a plan for what you intend to do once you finally hit the road and start moving toward your future.

I won't pretend to hide that this book focuses heavily on the contributions of HBCUs and the values, ideas, and examples that they offer people from all walks of life. I especially hope that in reading these chapters, you have found some inspiration and ideas that will propel you toward new beginnings in your life and career. I think it is essential to consider your values, your time, your feelings, and your legacy, especially when you are gearing up to make changes for the better. You are always welcome to shift into a lifestyle that best reflects who you want to be, how you want to feel, and what you hope to leave behind. Afford yourself the chance to change by planning for the life you truly desire.

Considering your values means considering what kinds of ideals you want your life to uphold and the things that you want to stand for. These things can always shift as necessary, but the goal is to find and establish the values that matter to you, and to live by them. We are living in a society that has certain embedded inequalities and ideals. These embedded narratives are not always healthy, and do not always promote well-being for everyone. We internalize these value systems though they are harmful for our self-esteem, our health, and the well-being of our families and communities. What use is it for me to believe racist ideas about Black people? What benefit do I have in upholding inequality in the workplace, when my freedom is inextricably tied to the freedom of others? Think about the ways that your values show up in your work and life and ask yourself seriously, *How can I shift my values and mindset for the better right now?* Not everyone is able to consider how their values may be upholding harmful and racist ideas. Whether you are a young student stepping foot on an HBCU campus for the first time or a seasoned professional seeking to turn over a new leaf, life is offering you the opportunity to reconsider what you have been taught to believe. Reflect upon the African American legacy and values of self-empowerment and excellence that are always accessible. These are not at all confined to the boundaries of an HBCU, and they never were.

When you are starting out on a new journey, consider how you want to feel. Feelings have long been a luxury that many Black folks don't allow themselves to factor into their work and lives, but your emotional state is important! I say often that life is about choices, and the choices you make should take into consideration your talents, needs, interests, and happiness. Does anyone really want a job that they hate and view as a burden to get up and go to every morning? Will that extra compensation contribute to a life well-lived? Your family and community will suffer if you are suffering, and your well-being is an important part of your being able to contribute to society and fulfill your purpose and goals. We are not always taught to keep happiness at the fore when making wise decisions, but when we're in the process of resetting our lives, often it is because unhappiness is the underlying cause. If something is not working, take the time to examine why and make the conscious effort to reset your emotional state while you shift your life and perspective. There is no point in taking poor emotional health or a negative attitude into a new chapter of your life. Contemplate your happiness and devise a plan that doesn't leave your joy behind.

The legacy you leave behind with your life and work can be a powerful motivating factor for change. Decisions to be better, to advance, to shift our mindsets and to focus on what is most important have ripple effects not only on ourselves but on all the lives we touch and interact with. Who would we be as a human race without the conscious choices of leaders who decided to live wholeheartedly within their purpose? What kind of inheritance will your life be for someone who comes after you?

CHAPTER 10

JOY

Gratitude: Cultivating Joy

Being joyful and maintaining that joy is its own measure of success. When I think about joy, and what it means to have a love for life, I think of my wife, my family, my friends, and the beautiful educational communities I have had the honor of being part of throughout my life. These things are part of what makes my life worth living, and I truly could not imagine who I would be without family and community. Yet, what strengthens my gratitude is also knowing that these things and the positive influences they have had in my life should not be taken for granted. The blessings of my life are not purely of my own making, and this inspires me with gratitude. Over the years, I have come to understand that joy starts from within, and happiness is not bound up in material possessions, though some might try to convince you otherwise. No matter our status or background, we can all develop a lasting love for life when we hold onto gratitude in all circumstances.

I'm not the first to say it and I surely will not be the last: Gratitude is a powerful indicator of joy. A grateful person can always find one more thing to be happy or feel positively about. A grateful person is always looking to express that gratitude and share it with other people. I am thankful for the many blessings that God has bestowed upon me, and being active in this gratitude has truly made my life better. Active gratitude can change a person's entire day. You can go from grumpy, overwhelmed, anxious, and unmotivated to optimistic, calm, and energized simply by cultivating and maintaining an active sense of gratitude. Just taking a moment to think about what is going right, and what we can be thankful for can be a great tool for regulating our thoughts and stress. It can make all the difference in your day-to-day, and over time it can change the way you see your life and purpose. Remember, gratitude is a virtue!

Don't Let Anyone Steal Your Love for Life

Joy is priceless, unquantifiable, and undefinable. Because of this, I think it is one of the most powerful resources we have at our disposal. I often think of infants and young children who laugh and squeal for seemingly no reason. Sometimes, they giggle without stopping just from a song or a silly game of peek-a-boo. The silliest and most nonsensical things can send a child into a fit of joy! We don't try to stop young ones from laughing or expressing their joy, even if we can't see the reason for their giggles and smiles. Just because we don't understand the reason for their joy doesn't mean we try to stomp it out. So, why do we do this to ourselves? Why do we undermine our own joy by trying to rationalize our feelings of happiness?

I was speaking to a young person the other day about an exciting opportunity she was pursuing. She had applied for a prestigious music fellowship and was waiting to hear back from the admissions committee regarding her acceptance.

"I'm so delighted for you," I told her. I was truly proud of her for having the courage to believe in herself, and to put her work out there in such an open way.

"Thank you," she said with a bashful smile, "but I don't want to get too excited!"

"Why not?" I replied. I could see the way her eyes lit up when she talked about the fellowship and her hopes for her career were evident. Even if she had yet to hear back about the results of her application, she deserved to feel pride, excitement, and joy.

"Don't rob yourself of your joy," I told her. "Use this excitement to fuel yourself to the next thing, and be proud of everything that you have already so wonderfully accomplished."

This is advice that I think everyone ought to hear. When you feel excitement, do not deprive yourself of that excitement. When you feel joy, when you feel gratitude, when you feel gladness or pride in yourself and your work, cherish these feelings and harness them to the best of your ability. Love your life and try your hardest to keep doubts, fears, and "haters" from undermining that love.

I'd be lying if I pretended that there aren't obstacles to joy out there. This world can be a devastating and overwhelming place to live in, in big and small ways. There are people out there who thrive on jealously, cruelty, unkindness, and stealing joy from others. Sometimes, the devil just has his fun sending these folks out to do his work. I am reminded of a story an HBCU graduate once told me about his experiences in corporate finance. Despite working on teams for long stretches of time, and receiving excellent reviews of his work, some team members simply refused to call him by his given name. They shortened it, changed it up, and remixed it in calls, meetings, and emails. Wouldn't that just ruin your day? The common courtesy of calling someone by the correct name is just one small but meaningful way to let a person know that you are in the very least acknowledging their presence and paying attention.

Be it microaggressions or macroaggressions, inhospitable environments in the workplace can get in the way of our success and make it hard for us to persevere through challenging situations. Yet, I know that if we are grounded in who we are and firm in our commitment to maintaining joy in our lives, we will be more equipped to handle aggression, jealously, cruelty, unkindness, and low-life behavior in the workplace and inequality in the world.

The Joy of Community

One of the greatest joys of an HBCU experience is the joy of gathering. In all the various ways that this gathering happens, there is something special that we create when we come together to celebrate, remember, and learn from one another. It may be the everyday competition at the spades table on the yard, or the lively, accented chatter of an international student event. It can be the sound of steppers and strollers on a Friday afternoon, or the song of graduated fraternity brothers returning to campus for an important anniversary. It can be homecoming or convocation, or any number of different occasions that bring us into communion with one another. The joy remains powerful, year after year, and it is fueled by our desire to be together as a community and family of people.

This joy of gathering is not at all reserved for an HBCU experience. It is as old as time and can be seen throughout history as a significant facet of Black culture and survival, from revival-era religious gatherings to the modern cookout or family reunion. There is joy to be had in being together and showing appreciation for one another through presence and community. Take joy in gathering with your chosen community and be intentional about coming together with others.

All too often, especially when we enter competitive work environments and become focused on career and achievement, we forget this important aspect of our lives. We are also conditioned to place less importance on solidarity with other Black folks and people of color when working in industries that lack diversity. There is an implicit understanding that we must compete with one another to have individual success. This is just another way that joy is robbed from us, as well as important power in community. Connect with the people around you and show up to community gatherings with the intention to participate in a love for one another, and a love for life.

The Role of Joy in Your Success

There are many ways to enjoy success, but there is no success greater than joy. You will know you have found success when you find yourself joyful and full of love for life. After all, being miserable isn't an indicator of a life well lived, is it?

Joy is not something that has to have a reason, so much as it must have an intention. If you want to laugh, you can find something to make you laugh, and if you want to smile, you can find a reason to smile. There is no rule saying that when things go bad you must be downcast, and there is no rule that says you must be joyful when life is going "perfectly." Funnily enough, I'm sure we can all remember a time when things were going well on the outside but not too great in our personal, emotional, or spiritual lives. Likewise, when we are going through tough or challenging times, it is still possible to be happy and bring gratitude into our vision. In fact, joy can be the very thing that pulls us through difficult situations or what fuels our passions in a positive way.

It is our perspective that makes all the difference when it comes to being joyful and maintaining a love for life. This is not to say that we don't need time to go through tough emotions or mourn disappointments and losses. As often as we can, we should choose to find the joyful way of living. As award-winning singer and songwriter India.Arie says, "It doesn't cost a thing to smile. You don't have to pay to laugh. You better thank God for that."

CHAPTER 11

BE YOURSELF, AND BELIEVE IN YOURSELF

It is impossible to believe in yourself if you are not even being yourself. When we walk through this world, we are often asked, forced, demanded, or expected to wear masks and fit into roles that do not match who we are inside. We are taught that we must hide our true opinions, make ourselves small, and adhere to the script written out by society. Sometimes the forces holding us to these expectations are external, from societal structures, institutions, and industries that we may be part of. Other times, the forces are closer to home, from our family, friends, and community. In any case, these pressures can sometimes turn us into people that we don't want to be or are not meant to be. How can you believe in that person, when that person is not even the real you?

Transcending Race

The beauty of an HBCU experience is that it allows you to transcend racial barriers and explore your own identity. I know what you might be thinking, and I'm not making a case for transracial identity, or saying that race isn't a real and significant facet of the societies we live in. However, I do believe that there is something powerful about learning and working in an environment where race is not the determining factor in your success, and where your blackness is not considered a flaw or an asset, depending on who is sizing you up. In a predominantly Black space, you will not succeed by hiding behind the racial profile that has been predefined for you. Instead, you are invited to discover yourself, and be yourself authentically.

Exploring who you are, what your true talents are, and your special brand of excellence, will be invaluable to your successes in life. Nobody can do what you do, the way you do it. Furthermore, what makes you special and desirable to hiring boards and gatekeepers is not just that you fill a diversity quota, or because you are the "unique" perspective (read: the only brown face) in the room. You are a person of integrity; you have received a quality education, and you are imbued with the confidence and character necessary to tackle any task and challenge before you. You are an heir to a legacy of excellence and greatness.

You Are Not Alone

Our historically Black colleges are filled with brilliant minds—valedictorians, distinguished scholars, and trailblazing industry makers. These people come from many different places, from different social and economic backgrounds, from different regions in the United States and all over the globe. HBCUs have often been the site of powerful collaboration between people from all backgrounds and walks of life. There are a multitude of ways to be Black, to be African, and to be diasporic. What you learn at an HBCU is that you do not have to conform to any models for what blackness is, because such stereotypes and molds could never encapsulate the fullness of the Black experiences that exist in the world.

For many students at HBCUs, this is one of the first most striking realizations. Blackness comes in different shades and sizes, different languages and traditions. Different values and understandings, different textures, flavors, and histories. There is a place for every kind of person on this planet, including whoever you may be, with all of your unique interests, ideas, and complexities.

This is demonstrated in the many ways that blackness is expressed on HBCU campuses, through clubs and interest groups, and in the melting pot of cultures that blend in our classrooms and dormitories. HBCU faculty likewise provide an impressive diversity of background and perspective. If you want to be a lawyer, engineer, or journalist, you can learn to be an excellent one. If you want to study foreign languages, film, and dance, you can become an expert in your field. If you want to travel abroad or toil in a laboratory, if you want to revolutionize public service or revitalize historical archives—if you want to change the world—you can. In our institutions of Black history and heritage, we are not shackled by our African identity or expected to perform a version of blackness that is palatable to others. We are liberated by the wholesale and unequivocal acceptance of our identity and heritage. With this in mind, it's important to ask yourself, Who might you be if you were free to be yourself?

You have been endowed with talent and a legacy. With an awareness of how precious that legacy is, you can move confidently in the world knowing that what makes you excellent has not been defined by what white history has allowed, but by what Black history has created.

It is also important to remember this when you are hired into a workplace or contributing to an endeavor where you might be "the only one." You may be "the only one" in the room but you are not the only one. You come from a lineage and tradition. You come from a long line of people who strive for excellence, develop their talents, and take them into the world. At any given moment in time all over this planet, there are Black people working for advancement in their fields, for justice, and for their families and communities. They are working individually and collectively, contributing to the future that new generations will one day inhabit.

Our History, Made by You

In this day and age, it is easy to become concerned with your individual life, and to miss the significance of collective and communal progress. The society we live in prioritizes personal achievement and asks us to divorce ourselves from the values and traditions that were so integral to our survival and success as a people. However, lessons learned from HBCUs are a sentinel of hope in this confusing age of individualism and collective apathy. Those who attend our schools, or consider the history of these strongholds for advancement, will be reminded of the significance of community in legacy building. You do not build a legacy for yourself. You build a legacy for your family, and for future generations. To consider your own legacy is to inherently consider the lives of others. How those people of the future are touched by the impacts of your life are determined by the way that you live today. In other words, your history is being made, today.

An example of this can be seen in the reputations of HBCUs among Fortune 500 companies, and others, that often hire HBCU graduates. Many HBCU business programs offer robust resources for their students and significant partnerships with top companies and employers across the nation and the globe. These companies make it their business to visit our schools, to be available for our students, and to provide footholds and incentives for the talent that they will be looking to hire in a few short years. Our capable, confident, and competent students attract these companies because they are well trained and hardworking. However, these relationships were not built simply through the brilliant insight of corporate entities. It is the alumni of our institutions who, after breaking barriers and executing world-class performance in their fields, forge relationships and secure opportunities for future generations of students. Meetings and lectures with industry executives, networking sessions, job fairs, and internship to entry-level hiring channels—these are the spoils of a hard-won battle for diversity and inclusion, led by conscious and trailblazing alumni. When our students leave our institutions, they make names not only for themselves, but for the institutions that trained them, and for the students who will rise through those same institutions for decades to come.

A Legacy for All

For a reader who has not attended an HBCU, this point I am making about the history of our schools may seem irrelevant to your daily life and future. You may wonder how there is value in learning about the opportunities you did not receive, or the experiences you did not have. Yet, I believe that the essence of an HBCU experience is more mutable and transformative than we realize at first consideration. What one learns at an HBCU is less about the specific period of attendance, and more about preparation for a future of success and the proliferation of a set of values.

At any moment, you have the power to embrace an empowering narrative about yourself and where you come from. Too often, we carry the burden of shame, of limiting beliefs and ideas that undermine our sense of agency and importance. We allow these things to affect our work lives and personal lives. We struggle to stand up, raise our voice, and speak out, simply because we are not practiced in advocating for ourselves, or we doubt our place to do so. Yet, every day is a new moment, and a new opportunity to change our perspective and release the beliefs that hold us back. Right now, you can think about ways to cultivate a deeper sense of self, and a stronger pride in your identity and heritage. Research the history and rest in the legacy of those who have come before you in your family, and in your field of work. Participate in community and seek always to engage with those around you in your neighborhood and workplace.

Think of these lessons learned as seeds of wisdom that can

be extracted and reproduced. Character-building values and lessons can be carried into new places and cultivated wherever you bring your talents and energies. If you remain open to new ideas, even if you are well past the moment of a collegiate experience, you can adapt the principles of Black excellence and upliftment at any moment in your life and career.

ACKNOWLEDGMENTS

A special thanks to Ms. Tracy Sherrod, my editor at Amistad Press, for suggesting that I write this book to share with the world the uniqueness of the historically Black colleges and universities (HBCU) experience and its tradition of producing exceptional graduates. Her advice and support were invaluable. My thanks also to Dr. Charrita Danley Quimby for assisting me with writing, editing, researching, and providing other support for this book. Ms. Carolyn Acklin deserves a special nod for her typing and retyping of the manuscript a number of times. I am grateful for the efforts of each of you.

To the hundreds of thousands of students and graduates of HBCUs as well as the administrators, faculty, and staff who ensure their successful operation, thank you for continuing to tell the HBCU story. It is a timeless story filled with historic places, magnificent accomplishments, and unparalleled achievements. Your individual and collective contributions to the nation and the world deserve recognition and commendations. May you always support and promote these national treasures.

ABOUT THE AUTHOR

Dr. William R. Harvey is an American educator, academic administrator, and businessman. From 1978 to 2022, he served with distinction as president of Hampton University and created a monumental legacy during his forty-four-year tenure—one of the longest tenures of any sitting president of a college or university in the country. After being named president, Dr. Harvey introduced innovations that solidified Hampton University's stellar position among the nation's colleges and universities. His commitment to excellence in academics resulted in ninety-two new academic programs, including twelve doctoral programs, being implemented under his watch. Other points of pride that occurred during his tenure as president include launching four weather satellites that are still in orbit, building the world's largest proton beam cancer treatment center, increasing the university's endowment from $29 million to over $400 million, and building thirty new structures, to name a few.

Over the course of his career, Dr. Harvey has been asked to serve on many for-profit and not-for-profit governing boards. Some of the for-profit corporate boards include Fannie Mae; First Union National Bank; Newport News Shipbuilding Corporation; Signet Banking Corporation; Pepsi-Cola Bottling

Company of Houghton, Michigan; and Trigon Blue Cross/ Blue Shield. The nonprofit boards are many and include National Geographic Society, National Collegiate Athletic Association (NCAA) Division I, National Merit Scholarship Corporation, Harvard University Graduate School of Education Alumni Council, Knoxville College Board of Trustees, Harvard Cooperative Society (COOP), University of Virginia Board of Visitors, Virginia Historical Society, Virginia Museum of Fine Arts, Woodrow Wilson Foundation Advisory Board, and the State Council of Higher Education for Virginia.

Dr. Harvey has also been appointed by six US presidents to such federal boards as the United States National Advisory Council on Elementary and Secondary Education, the Defense Advisory Committee on Women in the Service, the Fund for the Improvement of Postsecondary Education (where he served as chair), the National Association for Equal Opportunity in Higher Education (where he served as chair), the Commission on Presidential Scholars; the President's Advisory Board on HBCUs (where he served as chair), USO World Board of Governors, and the board of the US Department of Commerce's Minority Business Development Agency.

As a businessman, Dr. Harvey is well-respected. For forty years, he has been 100 percent owner of a Pepsi-Cola bottling plant in the state of Michigan. His well-known philanthropy is fueled by his business success.